Planting Design

Planting Design

Piet Oudolf and Noel Kingsbury

Gardens in Time and Space

TIMBER PRESS

Dedicated to the memory of Rob Leopold (1942-2005), garden philosopher, who played a crucial role in the development of the ecological garden movement in The Netherlands, and who went on to provoke and inspire discussion and debate beyond its borders. His sudden departure (presumably to replant the Elysian fields) as we were in the final stages of preparing this book has left us without one of our most open-hearted and open-minded colleagues.

Contents

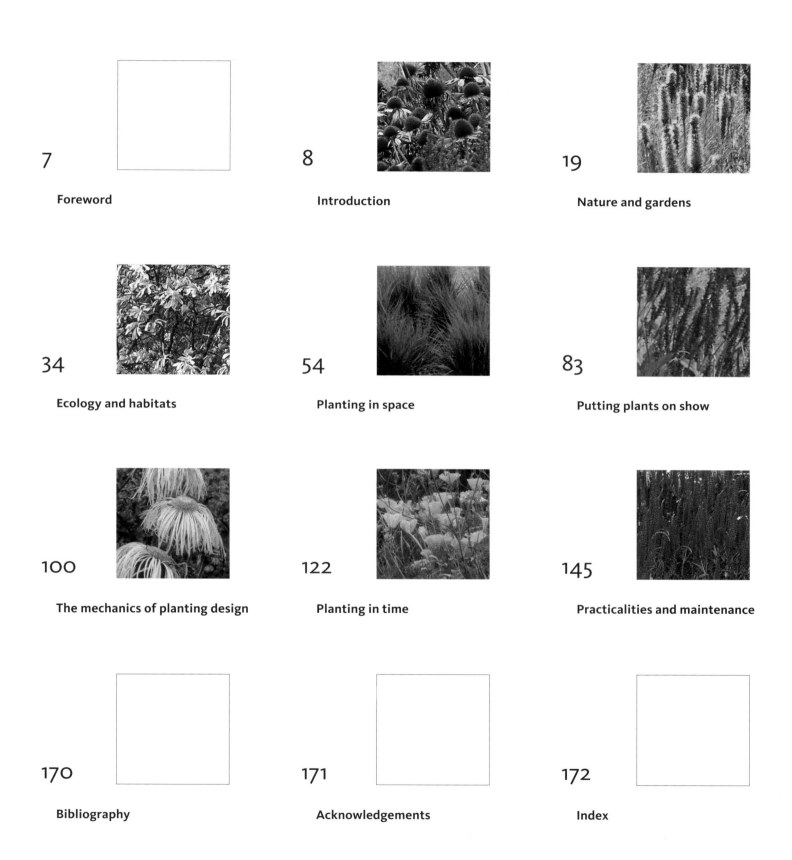

Foreword

Piet Oudolf, Noel Kingsbury and their colleagues in what has been called the New Wave planting movement have opened a door in the field of landscape architecture for the public realm.

The fields of landscape architecture and garden design are often confused by the public, but in the professional world they are two distinct areas of expertise. The former requires more urban and structural knowledge, but both benefit from detailed plant knowledge.

The task of landscape architecture in the public realm is vast, ranging from understanding natural systems to urban needs. Public landscape architecture has been driven by utilitarian, security and recreational needs. Yet the public flocks to garden shows and to historical landscapes that have extensive gardens with mixed borders and other floral displays. The opportunity to create new contemporary landscapes that offer this type of garden element to the public exists, yet most landscape architects have not used extensive herbaceous perennial plantings for public parks and gardens for reasons of lack of knowledge and the perceptions that they require extensive maintenance and that they are fragile.

Piet Oudolf's work is changing landscape architecture. His plant knowledge is exceptional and fascinating, his compositional talents magical. This is one of the most talented, sensitive designers of our time. In our collaboration on the Lurie Garden in Chicago, he was the creator of all the perennial plantings. As we worked on the overall composition, at times he was like an astounding plant mathematician. One could feel extensive plant knowledge flowing in his mind overlaid with artistic sensibilities. Each plant was an individual throughout the season, chosen not only for size, color and texture, but for transformation through time. He has the deepest knowledge of the plants' soil, water and light needs and is able to work in many different climates. Although there are many people with extensive plant knowledge, what Piet brings to this is his artistic vision, and an ability to translate that vision into dynamic combinations of plants that together create a total composition, one that is constantly changing throughout the season.

Noel Kingsbury has also addressed one of our major concerns, that of maintenance and durability. His work is particularly informative and the result of extensive research in new approaches in planting with minimum maintenance. Piet's collaboration with Noel has made his plantings remarkable for their resilience and longevity. They are planted in a manner that allows maintenance to be evolutionary, clear and coordinated.

As our society becomes more aware of the need for sustainability, we understand more the need for both native plants and for an ecological balance – both can play a part when we work with horticultural herbaceous perennials. Piet, Noel and their colleagues will be instrumental guides to our future.

Kathryn Gustafson
Landscape Architect

▼ Herbaceous plantings have always tended to look their best in late summer and autumn. The modern range, which includes many North American prairie species, is composed of robust and long-lived plants which reduces the maintenance traditionally associated with the herbaceous border.

Introduction

Planting is at the core of gardening and is central to the art of landscape design. During the twentieth century the greatest names in the history of garden and landscape art achieved their fame largely through their innovation and insight in the use of plants: Gertrude Jekyll, Vita Sackville-West, Mien Ruys, Roberto Burle Marx. Yet today, when gardening has become a huge industry attracting much media attention, planting design remains something of a poor relation to garden design. Meanwhile garden design has become too much like interior design applied out of doors, with a focus on overnight transformations rather than the craft of growing and nurturing plants. This book is an attempt to put the focus back on the art of planting.

We have written together before. Our book *Designing with Plants* (2000) was very much one of us (Noel Kingsbury) writing about the other's work (Piet Oudolf). Since then, much water has flowed under the bridge. Piet has taken on several large-scale and high-profile public planting projects as well as continuing his work for private clients; with his wife, Anja, he also runs a nursery which continues to grow in reputation. Noel, while continuing to work as a horticultural journalist and writer and developing plantings for a number of challenging public sites, has started a programme of research aiming at a more scientific understanding of garden plants; he is also working on a number of projects to link gardening with the wider intellectual and cultural world.

This book is first and foremost an account and an exploration of the authors' work – our work. Secondly it is a commentary on contemporary planting design inspired by nature and by ecology, where we look specifically at the work of those colleagues with whom we share space in something of a movement – not clearly defined enough perhaps to have a name, let alone a manifesto, but a movement nevertheless. Once again Noel is acting as the principal writer, but the book is about our shared vision and experience over the last decade. In it we hope to share our methods, discoveries and

▼ Large masses of grasses and perennials are a major feature of much contemporary planting design. Borders at the garden of the Royal Horticultural Society at Wisley, south-west of London, are a dramatic example.

Contemporary does not have to mean informal. Traditional skills such as the clipping of woody plants can serve modernist objectives, and their results make a dramatic contrast with more naturalistic plantings. ▼

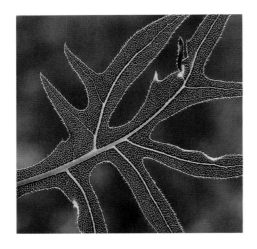

◄◄ Foliage may tempt one to closer inspection. Here the leaf of *Silphium laciniatum* is seen lit from behind.

◄ Shrubs and small trees are regarded by many as essential to parks and gardens. But the smaller the location, the more important it is that they provide plenty of interest. This is *Magnolia sprengeri*, with both flowers and fruit that are attractive.

thoughts with readers, be they amateur gardeners, landscape architects, garden designers, students or horticulturalists.

Perennials

We are largely concerned with herbaceous perennials. For us they are nature's chief ornament for the scale upon which we work, that of the garden. We also want to consider the city park: although this may be somewhat larger than the standard garden, we see it as a garden, and believe that it would be much better cared for if others saw it this way too. Some may think it odd that a book should be aiming to be as

relevant to park managers as it is to the owners of perhaps very small private gardens; but the basic principles of plant design and management are the same whatever the size of the plot – because the laws of nature, and therefore of ecology, apply to both. More pertinently, the division between people who garden for love and those who garden for a living is not as clear cut as it used to be. Citizen involvement in the management and sometimes in the creation of public parks is definitely on the increase, partly as a result of a greater desire on the part of people to play a more proactive role in their local communities, but also because funding for public spaces has declined in many industrialized countries, and citizen participation has served to plug the gap. Involvement takes many forms, from 'friends of parks' groups who lobby and fund-raise to volunteers who engage in hands-on maintenance in community gardens. In all of these cases, people are combining the role of amateur gardener with a whole new set of roles, blurring the formerly watertight distinction between the public and private domain. We hope that this book will also be useful for everyone who works in this area.

Another reason why we concentrate on perennials is their time scale. Unlike trees and shrubs, perennials develop quickly – often forming a decent-sized clump in three

Geometry and order seem to be central to the human concept of the garden. It is a challenge to a new generation of garden designers to develop plantings which recognize this without repeating the clichés of the past. ◄ The garden of Piet and Karin Boon, with massed grass *Deschampsia cespitosa*, and ▼ the Oudolf garden, Hummelo, both in the Netherlands.

► Many managers of public space lament the small amounts of money they are allocated. But Stefan Mattson, director of parks in Enköping in Sweden, has shown how it is possible to create extensive and beautiful plantings with an average budget. The 'Dreampark', designed by Piet Oudolf, is particularly successful, with its massed *Salvia nemorosa* and *S. xsuperba* varieties making a particularly striking feature.

▲ New public spaces, such as the Millennium Park in Chicago, offer great potential in improving the quality of life in the modern city. Perennials are ideal for such developments as they combine being long-lived with plenty of seasonal interest. Chicago is a good example of a city which has made a political decision to promote public green and ecological issues.

years – and so are ideal for creative gardeners who want to experiment and who enjoy making changes to their gardens in search of new or better artistic effects. It is less emotional to remove a perennial than a tree, and there is less risk and effort involved in moving them. In particular, the way they give such quick results makes them ideal for those increasing numbers of people who move house (and garden) frequently. Even in a relatively small garden it is possible to have a good variety, and they develop at a rate that satisfies both our impatience and our desire for continuity, since most are relatively long lived. It is possible for a small selection of the right varieties to be in flower from late winter to late autumn, while attractive foliage and distinctive structure can keep our interest for even longer.

A concentration on perennials does not mean that we are not interested in trees and shrubs (or annuals, bulbs and climbers). This book will include discussion of these other plant-growth forms, while maintaining the central focus on perennials. After all, most perennial plantings need a context, for which woody plants are essential and in which annuals and bulbs help fill the gaps. In particular, we want to look at how woody and herbaceous plants relate to one another over time. Their mutual relationship is essentially a dynamic one, the occupation of space and time by different plant forms changing constantly, both cyclically through the seasons and developmentally over the years.

Time and space

Time and space define all existence, and gardening and landscape design are arts that depend upon a more thorough exploration of time and space than perhaps any other. Most works of visual art (paintings, sculpture, architecture) are finished when the artist has completed them – from then on, they either stay the same or gradually deteriorate (or rather more rapidly in the case of some contemporary architecture which has pushed the boundaries of technology too far). Time-based art forms and media (film, drama, music) start and finish within a certain, more or less fixed time frame, and essentially repeat every time they are performed. Gardens are different – because they use a living material, which has its own agenda. When a designer 'signs off' a garden, it is not complete, but looks empty and raw. Even when the plants in the garden have grown to the size the designer envisaged, it is difficult to say whether the garden is actually 'finished' or not. Planting a garden is the beginning of an ongoing, unidirectional process which is impossible to start all over again. The design and creation of gardens is inextricably linked to the activity of gardening, as only active gardening has any hope of ensuring that the designer's vision is realized.

Much of the recent flurry of interest in garden design in both Europe and North America has unfortunately not been accompanied by an equal amount of interest in how gardens develop through time. This is perhaps inevitable when many of the new garden designers are more interested in paving, decking and the other inanimate aspects of garden-making. We adopt a very plant-centred approach.

We aim here to look at both the design and the maintenance aspects of planting. We argue that design and management are closely interlinked, so the best gardens are those which are created by people who combine the role of designer and gardener, or at least have an input and involvement with the management process. Consequently,

▶ Daylilies (*Hemerocallis*) are one of many groups of flowering perennials which are highly regarded by gardeners. The number of cultivars is truly vast, however, and gardeners who wish to use them need to consider not just issues about colour and size but also their suitability to different environmental conditions and their general resilience.

▶▶ Autumn colour like that displayed by this *Prunus* species is an important aspect of woody plants, and a major reason for including them in plantings. The colour is often brief, but it is regarded as an important marker of the changing seasons.

◄ Innovative planting often involves creating unexpected juxtapositions, such as pleached limes, associated with traditional garden styles, with grasses and loose perennial planting. In this planting by Dan Pearson, a thyme lawn is a particularly colourful feature.

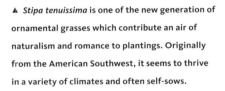

▲ *Stipa tenuissima* is one of the new generation of ornamental grasses which contribute an air of naturalism and romance to plantings. Originally from the American Southwest, it seems to thrive in a variety of climates and often self-sows.

The real test of a garden is how it looks in winter, when the bare bones of the design are revealed. Clipped woody plants, evergreen or deciduous, now come into their own. This is the Oudolf family garden in Hummelo. ▲

we see ourselves as addressing the designer as a gardener, and the gardener as a designer.

How one deals with spaces in gardens is a reflection of an attitude to plants, and this is where we sometimes find ourselves parting company from some of our colleagues. Landscape design has often used plants as filler material, vegetation to be stuffed into pre-allotted spaces with very little attention given to creative plant selection or combination. A design that is plant-focused is perhaps more inclined to design spaces around particular plants or plant combinations, which can lead to a radical rethinking of traditional ways of using space in the landscape. More plant-centred design can also encourage a reconsideration of some traditional forms in the garden, in particular that of the border, a legacy of the British (or perhaps more accurately English) tradition. Given how plant-centred much British gardening is, it is surprising how unadventurous British gardeners have been in developing new ways of displaying plants; in particular they have made endless repetitions of the rigid border format for so long that it has turned into something of a cliché. Designers elsewhere have often been more radical: Mien Ruys in the Netherlands, Roberto Burle Marx in Brazil and Wolfgang Oehme and James van Sweden in the USA. In this book we look at some contemporary approaches to the spatial arrangement of plants which we hope will inspire yet more radical thinking.

Nature and ecology

No artist, and certainly no scientist, works in isolation. We are both conscious of belonging to a movement, one which sees the future of planting design as being very much concerned with ecology, both as a science and as an aesthetic ideal. Nature for us remains the most fundamental inspiration. It is an important part of the current *Zeitgeist* that gardening is based on a sympathy with nature and an understanding of natural processes – which has not always been the case. Much energy is currently expended in arguing for a variety of positions which supposedly bring horticulture (and indeed landscape design) more in tune with nature – the organic and the native-plant

▼ Wild-plant communities, such as prairie, are an inspiration for many contemporary designers. This inspiration is not just aesthetic, but also very practical, as by understanding plant ecology we can learn much about management.

▼ Ornamental grasses can make a striking matrix, dominating a planting, with flowering perennials added for emphasis. The red spikes here are *Trifolium rubens*, the spires on the left *Digitalis ferruginea*.

Sporobolus heterolepis is a grass of the drier end of the prairie spectrum, the so-called 'short-grass prairie'. A knowledge of the habitats from which cultivated plants come can provide invaluable information about how they should be used in gardens and designed landscapes. ▼

movements are the two obvious ones. Both are inspired by philosophies or belief systems, and as such both deserve the rigorous attention of the critical mind. We are basically pragmatists, but will take seriously the concerns raised by these movements.

On the subject of ecology and nature, we have three points to make. All are at the core of what we do, and all are arguably topics which do not receive as much attention from those concerned with growing and using plants as perhaps they should.

WILD PLANT COMMUNITIES ARE A SOURCE OF INSPIRATION | Gardeners and designers all too rarely study nature for ideas, both aesthetic and practical. We both love looking at familiar and unfamiliar plants growing wild and believe that we can learn a great deal from asking how and where they grow. The widely recognized success of German practitioners in developing some of the most beautiful plantings of recent years owes a lot to the attention paid to the study of wild plant communities (*Pflanzensoziologie*) over more than a century. The work of Beth Chatto in Britain has also drawn more on the study of plants in the wild than has been realized, largely through the researches of her late husband Andrew on the wild origins of garden plants.

WE NEED TO KNOW MORE ABOUT HOW GARDEN PLANTS BEHAVE ECOLOGICALLY | Gardeners and designers know remarkably little about how the plants we grow in our gardens actually behave ecologically – how they compete for space, spread themselves around, how long they survive and so on. An understanding of these issues has considerable implications for the management of plantings, particularly more naturalistic ones. Here we aim to outline some of the issues and demonstrate how a basic understanding of plant ecology can inform the practice of planting design and garden management.

17

► Small gardens present a particular challenge to the designer. Domestic environments in particular require carefully designed 'hard' features to be balanced against the softness of planting. Here a carpet of low-growing perennials makes an effective feature of interest, but does not compromise a feeling of openness and space.

HUMANS ARE PART OF ECOLOGY, TOO | Some members of the ecology lobby speak and act as if ecology is somehow separate from *Homo sapiens*, going on from this to pronounce that only locally native plants are appropriate for use in many environments. But we have needs, too – one of which is for an attractive environment, in which ornamental planting clearly has an important role to play. We believe that there is little contradiction between providing a visually exciting environment for humans and making it wildlife-friendly. We would also point out that urban and many other environments are so unnatural that the best solutions for planting are often dictated not by what is 'native' but what grows best in an artificial setting.

Teamwork

The best parks and gardens are created through teamwork. This is true even of small gardens, where a couple have developed a garden together. The creation of larger projects involves people with many different skills working together, each recognizing that they understand some areas well but need to defer to others where they have less expertise. In such situations, one profession is not privileged over another, but each has something to contribute to a joint collaborative project. Teamwork is especially important in the increasing number of urban design projects where plants are being grown in conditions that are highly artificial – on roofs, for example. In such situations everyone concerned needs to be involved from the very beginning of the planning process.

Finally, we would stress the need for a teamwork approach with nature. The recognition of natural constraints on what we can do is reflected in current concerns over sustainability, but let us also develop an awareness of the incredible potential and adaptability that the world's flora offers us.

Nature and gardens

Gardeners and garden designers seek inspiration from a variety of sources. Among these, nature is perhaps a relatively recent choice, a reflection of changing attitudes to the natural world. Gardens have always held up a mirror to social and cultural attitudes to nature, and historically nature has been seen more as a foe than an ally. Past gardens were more about putting nature in its place within a human-led (but divinely sanctioned) plan than celebrating its diversity. Plants in the European classical garden tradition were ruthlessly clipped and ordered, shaped into geometrical forms and lined out in the landscape, becoming little more than green sculptural material in the process.

From the eighteenth century on, the natural in gardens has been celebrated more and more. The last hundred years has seen a variety of moves towards a style of gardening that seeks to re-create natural environments, to grow plants in a more 'natural' way or to learn something from nature in the way we use plants. It is not surprising now, at a time when we are acutely aware of how much damage the human race, both ancient and modern, has done to the natural world (and when some argue that environmentalism has become a new religion), that many want their gardens, parks and landscapes to be as 'natural' as possible. But can a garden ever be natural?

Here we wish to attempt to clarify some of the concepts and language used in much contemporary planting design.

Naturalistic and ecological aspects of design

Natural is a word that has become much misused. Heavily laden with ethical and ideological implications, it staggers under the burden. In a world where we are trying to mend our fences with nature, everyone, it seems, wants their ideas or their products to be natural. To be natural is to be good.

There are two ways of looking at prairie as a garden or landscape feature: one as aiming to reconstruct the complexity of the natural environment, the other producing a stylized version of it.

▼ At left a mass planting of the grass *Deschampsia cespitosa* with flowering perennials added. The catalpa trees evoke the savannah prairie of the American Midwest. At right is a wild prairie. ▼

19

In the garden it can also mean quite different things to different people. Before we proceed, it might be useful to discuss just how natural gardens, and more specifically planting design, can be. It is also important to stress here where this book, our work and the work of our colleagues, actually sits. We are all heavily influenced by approaches to garden-making that could be described as naturalistic or ecological, but we do not necessarily make gardens which are pure examples of either of these concepts. Interpretation of what is naturalistic also varies, as does the role of ecological process in gardens. We should point out that it is possible to have plantings which are naturalistic in appearance and ecological in the way that they function in the midst of gardens which are highly artificial – a meadow in a formal setting, for example.

Strictly speaking, nothing that is made by people can be truly natural, and since gardens (unless they are simply enclosures of wild landscapes) are by definition human artefacts, it is perhaps misleading to speak of natural gardens. Even when we choose to restore a habitat, it is our choice, a human choice, that we restore. Further confusion is caused by those who use *natural* interchangeably with *organic*, meaning a system of cultivation that eschews synthetic chemicals – which could mean that a formal rose garden could be deemed 'natural' if it was managed only by organic means. From now

◄ Wildflower meadow is a highly complex semi-natural
plant community which – as many have discovered – is
very difficult to emulate in the garden.
But it has inspired the creation of many borders that
use grasses and flowering perennials in a relaxed and
naturalistic way. ▲

on, we would prefer to speak of gardens which are inspired by nature and which aim at reproducing nature's outward forms as *naturalistic*.

While naturalistic refers primarily to the outward form – that is, the end result of design and process, *ecological* refers to process, or how the planting actually functions. Like natural, ecological is a feel-good term in a world where many have a sense of guilt about the human destruction of nature, so we need to agree a more precise definition. Traditionally, planting styles have used plants according to aesthetic and functional criteria. But recent decades have seen a number of ways in which planting design can be validly described as 'ecological', primarily to do with matching plants with their environment and with developing plantings where ecological processes are allowed a larger role than in traditional plantings.

Here, we wish to dissect and define the concepts of naturalistic and ecological in planting design. For us, in our practice, as with most of those who we see as colleagues in the naturalistic planting movement, these are *aspects* of our work. We do not wish to elevate them to the status of religious virtues or absolute truths. To put ourselves into a philosophical and political context, we are very definitely not part of the deep ecology movement – that wing of environmentalism which believes that humans have equal rights with nature, and no right to order nature. (These concepts are particularly linked with the activist group Earth First! and the writings of Norwegian philosopher Arne Ness.) Much of what we do is only partly naturalistic and sometimes not very ecological – but these two concepts always *inform* our work to a greater or lesser degree. As will be explained, we see them as being part of a continuum, a continuum which also includes the vision of the human artistic imagination.

First, the word *naturalistic*. The use of plants with wild character and nature-inspired planting patterns are two aspects which almost define the word:

USE OF PLANTS WITH WILD CHARACTER | Conventional horticulture has relied heavily on plants which are the result of years of selection and breeding, many with very artificial characters: double flowers, bright colours, variegated and tinted foliage, compact habit and so on. For more than a hundred years now, gardeners have been divided between those who rely heavily on such plants and those who rather dislike them, preferring to rely on wild species, or on those cultivars and hybrids which maintain much of the natural proportion and elegance of wild species. The English writer on aesthetics John Ruskin (1819–1900) and the Irish garden writer William Robinson (1838–1935) were two historic voices who are famous for their promotion of the natural over the hybrid.

NATURE-INSPIRED PLANTING PATTERNS | Over the last hundred years, there has been a definite attempt to make planting design less controlled and geometric, culminating in attempts to mimic, or at least learn from, the ways that plants combine in nature. With plantings that aim to be dynamic and ecological, this is absolutely inherent in the design intention, as the plants are effectively being allowed to choose their own places in the planting to a large extent. However, such a naturally driven order may not

Gardeners and designers may choose regionally native plants for a number of reasons, including the links they provide to local landscapes and their value to particular wildlife. These are both midwestern American prairie natives, *Geum triflorum* ▲ and *Silphium laciniatum* ▼.

always be seen by human onlookers as being desirable or aesthetically pleasing. Consequently, designers usually aim at visually attractive combinations that evoke nature – that are an idealized version of it – rather than directly copying it.

There is much less agreement over two other areas, the use of native plants and the role of clipping woody plants into geometric forms:

USE OF NATIVE SPECIES | Using plants native to a particular region has been a growing movement for many years now. It has become of great importance in the United States, while in the Netherlands it has been influential for several decades. Dutch practitioners tend to be relatively pragmatic, accepting almost as 'honorary natives' some well-established introduced species, whereas in the States there has

been much less willingness to do this. Those interested in these issues should read A.D. Kendle and J.E. Rose (2000), writers who – despite a lifelong commitment to ecology and the use of native plants – have argued for a pragmatic approach and the use of non-natives. Some, notably those who would describe themselves primarily as ecologists, regard the growing of natives as vitally important for biodiversity, and would argue that there is a clear moral imperative in doing so. Others, including most horticulturalists, would argue that native-only planting rarely delivers the quality of visual experience that human users of gardens and landscapes want. Research also seems to suggest that wildlife does not, in fact, necessarily benefit from such a restricted approach. A pragmatic synthesis is likely, with more gardeners using visually attractive locally native plants in their work, combined with introduced species. European gardeners in particular have relied heavily on perennials of North American origin for some two centuries now; so our discussion of prairie plantings should be little more than a logical next step for them.

AVOIDING FORMALITY | One of the greatest ongoing debates in garden and landscape design has been over the use of clipped trees and shrubs and the ordering of plants into highly artificial patterns. At times this has acquired a sinister nationalistic character, with writers like the German Willy Lange (1864-1951) and the Danish / American Jens Jensen (1860-1951) seeing naturalistic planting as being inherently 'nordic' and therefore superior to 'latin' formal planting. Formality is still regarded by many as anathema, particularly in the United States. It is worth pointing out, however, that although classical formality may appear 'unnatural', it is not necessarily anti-nature – do birds and butterflies really care whether food plants and nesting sites are in organic curves or straight lines?

Now, the word *ecological*. The first aspect, biodiversity, is agreed to be important by almost everyone. Two other aspects, ecological fit and dynamism, perhaps more truly define a planting as ecological:

BIODIVERSITY | Recent years have seen a growing awareness of the importance of gardens for wildlife, particularly in urban and suburban areas. Even if not managed particularly with wildlife in mind, gardens do provide a range of very good habitats, as J. Owen (1991) has shown. Indeed, they can support a higher level of biodiversity than intensively managed farmland. Gardens that are designed to be 'wildlife-friendly' can thus be said to be participating in the wider ecology.

ECOLOGICAL FIT | Much research in Germany (notably that led by Richard Hansen at the Weihenstephan institute in Bavaria) has focused on choosing plant species which will flourish in the prevailing conditions. The idea is to draw up a selection of species whose ecological requirements (for moisture, fertility and so on) match those of the given site. Less systematic, but more important in terms of propagating these ideas, has been the work of England's Beth Chatto, whose books and nursery have become widely known.

DYNAMIC PLANTINGS | The most sophisticated approach to ecological garden design concerns the development of plantings which effectively function as artificial ecosystems, comprising combinations of plants that show a high level of compatibility and so remain relatively stable with little maintenance. However, some natural processes are dynamic, so change is inevitable, with species populations ebbing and flowing. This dynamism is quite alien to conventional planting practice, where plants are expected to stay where they are put, but here it is accepted as integral to the design.

How are we to make sense of the variety of approaches to a more naturalistic and ecological planting style, to say nothing of occasional disagreements, which are being taken by today's garden and landscape designers? One possibility is to think of a gradient that runs from the formal to the wild:

Formal	Wild
control – maintenance ensures that a design is strictly kept	dynamism
clipping and shaping	plants allowed to develop natural form
limited range of species	wide range of species
human intention stressed	apparent spontaneity

Baroque gardens and nineteenth-century regimentation are clear examples of the formal end of the gradient. The middle of such a spectrum might include the twentieth-century style typified by Vita Sackville-West (1892-1962) and Gertrude Jekyll (1843-1932), where a structured framework enclosed informal border planting. Mien Ruys (1904-1998), the Bauhaus-trained designer who combined architectural features and rich planting, might also belong here. Applying this gradient to contemporary planting design, Piet Oudolf's work can also be seen as belonging to this central position. He combines certain formal elements with rich planting; plants with wild character

▲ Real prairie or meadow is a dynamic system, with plant populations changing every year in response to a variety of factors such as climate or animal predation. Management such as mowing, cutting or burning can also make a difference, benefiting some species but limiting others.

Eremurus cultivars are spectacular, but if we remain ignorant of their ecology we will probably fail with them. They are mountain-desert plants, and so need very good drainage, sun, and an absence of competition. This planting is designed by Dan Pearson. ▲

being a particular feature. This position may also suit the work of James van Sweden and Wolfgang Oehme, who – in their earlier, best known designs – used large masses of plants to create a strong visual impact. Their work in fact involves little that can be described as ecological, but gives the impression of being naturalistic because species with wild character are used and there are absolutely no formal elements.

Further on, towards the wild end of the spectrum, come a number of other designers who work more genuinely ecologically. Designers in Germany, facing a more extreme continental climate than their Dutch or British counterparts, have had to take more notice of the importance of achieving a good ecological fit between place and plant. A long history of the study of plant communities in German academic botany has further encouraged an emphasis on the ecological, with a greater acceptance of dynamism in plantings than has been acceptable in Britain or the United States. Consequently, the perennial-based planting schemes that can be seen in many public parks in Germany have a very naturalistic appearance, with little of the woody plant structure that other gardening cultures expect.

At the wildest end of the spectrum are those who work with habitats dominated by native plants, such as meadows or woodland, where natural dynamics are given a large hand in the ongoing development of the planting. Different species tend to dominate from year to year, and unless attempts are periodically made to reverse the process there is a definite succession, the changing of the original plant community to another, more stable one, with longer-lived and more competitive plants gradually displacing those that are quicker to establish and so predominate in the early stages.

Contemporary planting design

The use of regionally native plants is a major and growing aspect of much contemporary planting design. However, the aesthetic appeal of such species varies enormously from region to region, and is often not sufficient to make it possible to rely on native species alone for high-impact plantings.

▶ In nature, plants nearly always grow in complex intermingled combinations, such as in this prairie in Missouri.

In cultivation, however, we usually grow plants in blocks – the more artificial-looking the block, the more dramatic the result, as in this corporate planting designed by Piet Oudolf. The pink spikes are *Liatris spicata*. ▲

27

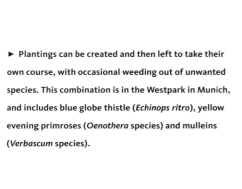

► Plantings can be created and then left to take their own course, with occasional weeding out of unwanted species. This combination is in the Westpark in Munich, and includes blue globe thistle (*Echinops ritro*), yellow evening primroses (*Oenothera* species) and mulleins (*Verbascum* species).

Oehme–van Sweden Associates is known for creating dramatic perennial-based plantings, often using monocultural blocks. Here, however, a more subtle intermingling comprising the grass *Deschampsia cespitosa* and the red *Monarda didyma* illustrates the continued development of the partnership's planting design work. ►►

A good example of how the native-plant movement is affecting more mainstream designers is that of Oehme-van Sweden Associates in the United States. Both Wolfgang Oehme and James van Sweden, the founders of this highly successful partnership, trained as landscape architects after originally studying in other disciplines – van Sweden as an architect and Oehme (who was born in Germany) as a horticulturalist. The two men have always been critical of the vast areas of sterile lawn and fiercely clipped shrubs that are such a feature of the American landscape. Instead they have used large drifts of ornamental grasses and perennials to create a quilted look, although in their private garden work they developed a much greater level of complexity. In their 'classic' work there was no intermingling of species, and much of the visual effect was gained from using large monocultural blocks. The practice is, however, now changing its approach to planting design, through younger project managers and partners developing their own style, which often involves a much greater use of native vegetation and more subtle intermingling of plant varieties.
In Britain, in private gardens, the designer Dan Pearson has also developed a distinct naturalistic style based on using plants which evoke the looseness and romance of wild places. His work successfully combines a natural look with the strong visual appeal that is often lacking when only native species are used. Keith Wiley's work is also highly regarded for its sophisticated approach to plantings inspired by natural habitats.

In the Netherlands, there has been a particularly strong movement towards growing native plants. The organization Oase (meaning oasis) is dedicated to the promotion of wildlife-friendly gardens rich in native species. A particularly fine example is the series of parks in the Amsterdam suburb of Amstelveen. Hein Koningen, who retired in 2002 as director of the town's green-space department, developed a style of planting which relied heavily on the recognition of the natural process of *succession* in wild-plant communities. Sensitive management over many years results in a patchwork of habitats – good for biodiversity, but also with considerable visual interest for the human visitor.

29

▲ Keith Wiley's plantings at the Garden House in Devon, England, involved encouraging a wide variety of species to self-sow, including the biennials seen here in early summer: mauve *Hesperis matronalis*, yellow *Oenothera biennis*, white umbellifer *Daucus carota* (wild carrot) and crimson *Lychnis coronaria*, as well as perennials such as blue *Campanula lactiflora*.

Those who manage areas of planting larger than the conventional domestic garden have a lot to learn from people like Hein who deal with semi-natural or managed vegetation. Only a limited amount of time (or money) can be invested in looking after large country gardens, public parks, highways or corporately owned landscapes. All too often such places are simply mown – an unimaginative solution which contributes little to the visual environment, practically nothing to biodiversity, and in terms of sustainability (fuel-guzzling and CO_2-producing mowers) can only be judged as irresponsible.

Other developments in the Netherlands have focused on the creation of naturalistic combinations of annuals, for example in the work of Rob Leopold, who for many years operated at the hub of a network involving the whole Dutch nature-planting movement. Henk Gerritsen's widely admired Priona Garden, which combined robust garden perennials and natives, has also been very influential.

Annual seed mixtures for use in parks and other public spaces have also been developed by Nigel Dunnett at Sheffield University in England. They have been a particular commercial success, being a cost-effective way for public-space managers to create very colourful displays that take only a few months to flower from a spring sowing. Nigel has also worked on an ornamental version of coppicing, the traditional European woodland management where trees are cut down to ground level on a cyclical basis to encourage the growth of new and generally very straight shoots. Ornamental coppice is a way of combining decorative woody plants with a herbaceous understorey, a strategy that can be managed using relatively unskilled staff.

Nigel Dunnett and his colleague James Hitchmough have advanced the concept of 'enhanced nature', the idea that what are essentially artificial ecosystems can be developed for urban areas, comprising both native and non-native species. James has also worked on prairie and on various other techniques of developing colourful 'wildflower-meadow' type plantings through both planting and the direct sowing of seed. He has also looked at the possibilities of getting perennial species to co-exist with grasses to form 'perennial meadows'. Relatively few species have the vigour to do so on fertile soils in the long growing season of the British climate, but the technique does have definite potential.

One of us, Noel Kingsbury, has research links with Sheffield, and works in a similar vein, developing perennial-based plantings for public spaces, particularly for spaces which are seemingly mundane (traffic islands, roundabouts and other roadside plantings), but which are seen by thousands daily. The varying techniques and

▲ Annuals, or perennials and annuals together, as here, make for particularly colourful combinations, popular with the general public. This is a large-scale scheme in a suburb of Sheffield, in northern England, created as part of an urban regeneration scheme.

▼ Silbersommer (silver summer) is the name of a particularly successful planting combination developed in Germany, primarily for dry calcareous soils. It starts off with bulbs in spring, followed by a variety of perennials flowering in early summer (the blue is *Linum perenne*) and it still looks good in winter. Structure is as important as colour in the overall effect created.

approaches used by the Sheffield School are essentially broad-brush – designed to create impact in large areas such as parks, highway verges or other extensive urban or semi-urban areas. There is a very clear emphasis on selecting plants on the basis of aesthetics as well as ecology, but the visual impact is very much dependent upon seeing large expanses of planting or seeing it in a wider context, rather than close-to or in small spaces. In this respect it is similar to the developing field of 'mixed planting' in Germany, which is also designed to look at its best when seen at a glance in its totality rather than scrutinized closely.

Mixed planting is the latest manifestation of the very impressive, and strongly research-based, work on planting design which has been taking place in Germany. In mixed planting a list of species is devised for a particular site containing a fixed proportion of each species or variety. The plant list is selected on both ecological and aesthetic criteria. The idea is that plants can be bought for a particular area, the number being calculated on an area basis, and which then can be planted at equal distances at random by relatively unskilled personnel. There is little doubt that the scheme works aesthetically only on a large scale, but also that at least one mixture, Silbersommer (silver summer), designed for dry alkaline soils, does look absolutely spectacular. The 'integrated planting system' is similar, but includes bulbs and annuals as well as perennials, and at least one of the mixtures, Sommernachtstraum (summer-night's dream), developed by Hochschule Wädenswil (an educational and research institution, in Switzerland), is being commercially marketed (Föhn, 2004).

Such formulaic planting combinations offer the opportunity for clients such as local government to buy and install plantings without the expense of employing a designer. However, they may well need skilled maintenance if the schemes are to develop over the years as harmonious and balanced plantings.

The origin of these planting styles lie in what could be termed *Lebensbereich* planting. The word refers to a specific 'living space' within a park or garden, a sub-habitat, and illustrates the centrality of matching plant with environment which has been central to planting design in Germany over the latter half of the twentieth century, and which has resulted in many striking plantings in public parks.

Interest in 'prairie' has also been growing in Germany. This is an attempt to address an underlying problem, which to the conventional gardener may seem like a rather counter-intuitive one, that of soil fertility. The most floristically diverse and visually rich temperate-zone European wildflower habitats are those of dry limestone soils, whereas moist fertile soils are prone to develop species-poor communities of aggressive pasture grasses and weedy species such as nettles and docks. Where low-maintenance natural-looking plantings are wanted, few European natives are actually able to compete, hence an interest in using North American prairie plants, which by nature are generally species of fertile soils and thus possibly better able to compete with the aggressive local weeds. Cassian Schmidt, the current director of Hermannshof in Weinheim in the Rhine valley, a leading German experimental garden, is very much at the forefront of these developments.

Partly as a consequence of these experiments, the term *prairie* in Europe has taken on a broader meaning than North Americans would recognize – often it is applied to any nature-inspired planting of large perennials and grasses. It is early days yet to see what will become of this particular trend. At the very least it should result in the introduction to wider cultivation of many more good species and cultivars.

▼ **Lady Farm in Somerset, created by owner Judy Pearce with the advice of Mary Payne, a teacher of horticulture, is a striking example of contemporary planting influenced by continental European approaches. At midsummer species and cultivars of *Kniphofia*, *Achillea* and *Verbascum* mix well with grasses *Stipa gigantea* and *S. tenuissima* and the sedge *Carex comans*.**

▲ Herbaceous plants can be used to create contrast with very formal plantings. Here a border of grasses (*Miscanthus* and *Molinia* cultivars) and *Eupatorium purpureum* subsp. *maculatum* 'Atropurpureum' counterpoints a severe combination of yew and *Deschampsia* grass. This is the garden made for Piet and Karin Boon, The Netherlands. Design: Piet Oudolf.

Key to these more ecological approaches to planting design is the acceptance of an essential dynamism, of the inevitability of change; plants are going to move around as some die out and others self-seed or send out runners. Such an acceptance of dynamism means that not every piece of every planting is always going to be perfect – the element of control that is expected of more conventional or design-led plantings simply is not there. In any case, this level of control is unrealistic for urban environments where plantings are subject to a variety of vicissitudes, including children on bikes and the depradations of dogs – aside from low-quality management.

This is a good place to stress the distinction between a dynamic, more ecologically driven style and the more design-led approach of Oehme-van Sweden and Piet Oudolf, where there is more emphasis on precision, of particular plant combinations with a particular spatial configuration being maintained over time, and a varying, and generally reduced, tolerance of plants moving around within the planting.

▼ Cultivars of *Veronicastrum virginicum* are very effective as ornamental herbaceous plants and flourish in a very wide range of climates. However, they can be slower to establish than many herbaceous plants, which the designer needs to be aware of when planning a planting.

Ecology and habitats

In the first chapter we looked at various approaches to so-called natural or ecological planting design. Here we will look at some of the issues raised by plant ecology and their implications for gardeners. It is important to stress that *all* gardeners and designers should pay more heed to plant ecology, not just those who are interested in naturalistic design, wildlife gardening or growing native species. There are two main sets of reasons for this – to do with plant selection and with maintenance. A better understanding of some basic ecological principles can inform our practice in both areas, which is of as much relevance to a formal garden as a wild one.

Plant selection and climate

Climate has a great influence on plant selection. In areas such as north-western Europe, a maritime climate ensures that summers are rarely hot, winters rarely cold and there is plentiful year-round rainfall. This makes it possible to grow a very wide range of plants, considerably more than in areas of continental climate where hotter summers (with often less certainty of rainfall) or colder winters limit what can be grown. However, even those areas which experience mild maritime temperatures do not always have year-round rainfall; for example, much of the North American Pacific Northwest experiences long summer drought, which can be a major limiting factor on what can be grown.

For the designer, the possibility of growing a wide range of plants makes it possible to bring together species from a very wide range of habitats – typically boreal, alpine, cool temperate, Mediterranean, montane and sub-tropical. Since plant form often reflects habitat (for example, many plants of dry-summer climate have silvery leaves), this means that the designer's plant palette is very wide and a great many contrasting forms and textures can be brought together. Those who design gardens and landscapes in climates which impose greater limitations on what can be grown will inevitably work with a narrower plant palette and consequently a narrower range of aesthetic possibilities.

Gardeners in relatively severe climates do not need telling that they are limited, but those in 'soft' climates can sometimes become complacent; there are a number of reasons why they should perhaps pay more attention to plant selection issues:

CLIMATE CHANGE | Whether or not climate change is natural or human-induced, there is little doubt that many regions are experiencing warmer weather – either hotter summers or less cold winters. On the one hand this can increase the potential for less hardy plants to be grown, but it also increases the likelihood of potentially damaging droughts.

WATER | People in many areas are accustomed to using irrigation as a matter of course. We cannot assume that this will always be the case, as our use of water is profligate and arguably unsustainable. In the future it may not always be safe to plan gardens with the assumption that irrigation will always be available.

35

URBAN AND ARTIFICIAL ENVIRONMENTS | Gardeners and landscape designers in urban areas often have to contend with soils which have been damaged by up to centuries of abuse. Such soils may be thin, full of rubble, low in moisture- and nutrient-retaining humus, or very alkaline through containing a high proportion of cement products. They are generally low in nutrients and have a greatly reduced ability to hold moisture. Increasingly, too, gardens are being made in artificially constructed soils, on roofs or over subterranean constructions. Here there is no natural water table for plants to draw on in drought, and while in many such situations there may be a dependable irrigation system, this may not always be the case.

Given these issues, it is worthwhile for designers in even the most forgiving of climates to pay more attention to how to select plants for difficult conditions – summer drought in particular.

Plant survival strategies

One of the potentially most useful concepts to come out of the science of plant ecology is that of survival strategies. The work behind this concept – discussed by J. P. Grime (2001) – argues that plants employ three basic strategies to survive, or at least to ensure the survival of their genes and therefore the species if not themselves. All plants, it is argued, show a combination of these three strategies in greater or lesser amounts. The concept of survival strategies also explains a lot about the rationale behind many garden practices.

The three basic strategies define plants as competitors, stress-tolerators and ruderals. It should be noted that these terms are used here in a precise scientific sense, and may differ from their everyday usage.

COMPETITORS | thrive in high-resource environments with plenty of light, moisture and nutrients, and a reasonably long, or warm, growing season. Those that survive are those which can make most effective use of these resources – can grow fastest, reproduce effectively, move into vacant space and out-compete surrounding plants. They tend to:

be tall — to get to the light

grow fast — to occupy space

be able rapidly to extend shoots sideways — to occupy newly vacant areas

have large soft foliage — to shade out other plants

flower relatively late — because establishing territory comes first

Competitive plants thrive on moist and fertile soils, establish rapidly, tend to look lush and luxuriant, and produce a lot of dead material by the end of the season – an important maintenance point to remember. It makes sense to use them in high-resource environments, but there is a strong tendency for diversity to decline over time. Simply because this is a 'winner-takes-all' situation, some species will be out-competed and die out. This clearly has implications for both design and maintenance.

ECOLOGY AND HABITATS

Trifolium rubens in the wild in a meadow in
Slovenia ▼, and in cultivation ▼. Plants in cultivation
often have a different habit to those in the wild,
generally being larger and looser. In both cases,
though, they look highly effective next to grasses.

Plantings which are very intermingled maximize the interface zone and hence the competition between species, so that the most vigorous could end up eliminating the others. Growing plants in blocks reduces the interface between species and makes it easier for people responsible for maintenance to reduce the size of the most vigorous. However, it is often possible to combine competitive plants in more visually complex intermingled plantings if the quantity and quality of maintenance is good enough, with only the most competitive species grown in monocultural blocks. An enormous advantage of competitive plants is that they stand a decent chance of out-competing weeds, and are therefore invaluable for low-maintenance situations.

STRESS-TOLERATORS | Where resources are low, plants have to conserve them. Low-resource factors such as shade, seasonal drought, poor soil, soil containing toxins (natural or caused by pollution) and waterlogging all reduce a plant's ability to absorb nutrients, so it is not surprising that the storage of nutrient reserves is a key feature of stress-tolerant plants. They tend to:

grow slowly — to conserve resources
have tough evergreen leaves — to conserve energy, and to make them unpalatable to predators
have small leaves and be physically tough — to reduce damage and therefore loss of resources
flower early rather than later — to ensure that genes are passed sooner

Since there are many different stresses, there are many different adaptations, with consequences for a very different physical appearance. Among the most familiar are:

shade — deep green evergreen leaves maximize photosynthesis

drought — small, grey or bronze leaves; coatings and shape minimize moisture loss spines, aromatic oils discourage predation

salt — grey leaves; waxy coating reduces desiccation

wind — very small or linear leaves reduce physical damage and desiccation

Many of these adaptations are what makes a plant aesthetically pleasing – thus the silver-grey of lavender, the aromatic smell of sage and the neat hummocks of alpine hebes all aid tolerance of drought or exposure.

A great many plants of stressful habitats are, more correctly, stress-avoiders. Bulbs and other geophytes are good examples: they avoid stress by growing at a time of year when they can maximize the scarce resources provided by winter sunlight coming through bare tree branches. Many herbaceous plants are summer-dormant in dry climate zones too, thus avoiding stress rather than tolerating it.

An awareness of the different kinds of stress-tolerant plants is clearly a boon to the gardener and designer, and the visual qualities of many of them are an added bonus. Because stress-tolerant plants tend to be slow-growing, it is possible to ensure a relatively high level of diversity in plantings; they are not so liable to out-compete each other, making intermingled plantings easy and often visually exciting. The amount of dead material at the end of the year tends to be low, so reducing maintenance.

Given the way that many stress-tolerant plants grow, there may often be gaps between plants, but these are less likely to be filled with weeds than in more resource-rich sites, as drought or other stresses will reduce the weeds' ability to compete with the desired plants. However, stress-tolerant plants are often used in situations where, strictly speaking, the stress is not so great, and the gaps can become vulnerable to invasion by weeds. Mulches of stone (as in gravel gardens) or woodchip (as in woodland plantings) help to reduce this.

RUDERALS (PIONEERS) | 'Live fast, die young' is the ruderal motto. Ruderals, or pioneers to use a more readily understood but informal term, are plants which are adapted by evolution to fill gaps, growing rapidly to flower quickly and then distribute large quantities of seed. This seed will often last for years in the ground, enabling the pioneers to establish themselves at once if the existing vegetation is removed and the soil disturbed. Pioneers tend to:

be rapid growing — to establish themselves before others

have showy flowers and flower over a long period — to make sure they get pollinated

produce large quantities of seed — to ensure gene survival

die young — because survival of the species is the important factor in habitats which are often unstable

▼ The more severe an environment, the more vital it is to select plants which are known to be suited to the conditions. Wild habitats are always a good place to see what will survive. Here sea-kale (*Crambe maritima*) and red valerian (*Centranthus ruber*) flourish in conditions which would rapidly kill most other plants.

ECOLOGY AND HABITATS

◄ Plantings of short-lived species can be very exciting, as they develop rapidly and tend to be very free-flowering. Here a variety of species makes a colourful midsummer combination, including *Foeniculum vulgare* 'Giant Bronze', the white annual umbellifer *Ammi majus* and the mauve short-lived perennial *Verbena bonariensis*.

Annuals and biennials are pioneers, as are many short-lived perennials and 'monocarps', those species which live for several years, flower spectacularly and then die. Some plant families have large numbers of pioneer species. The umbellifers (Apiaceae), for example, include many biennials and monocarps.

The first thing many gardeners think of when hearing about the pioneer strategy is 'weeds'. Many common weeds are pioneer species, and the old-fashioned practice of having large expanses of bare earth in the garden was just what they wanted – a perfect seedbed. Many pioneers, of course, are popular as annuals and other short-lived ornamental plants.

In perennial planting schemes, the pioneer strategy is useful. Plants that look good and produce a lot of seed which grows quickly can be depended on to fill any gaps that occur, scattering themselves around a planting, creating interest and, if carefully chosen, not seriously competing with long-lived species.

• *Understanding survival strategies*

The three strategies outlined here are rarely 'pure' – the vast majority of plants combine them, so they should be seen as means of understanding plant behaviour rather than as cut-and-dried categories. Ecologists use a variety of laboratory techniques to evaluate survival strategies, which sometimes give rather counter-intuitive results. Essentially, the strategy has to be seen as relative to the habitat, so that a plant which we might think of as a stress-tolerator in a garden setting – such as *Salvia nemorosa*, which always seems to thrive in a drought – acts as a competitor in its native dry-meadow habitat. Yet the whole concept is a very useful one for those concerned with plant selection and management, and we do not have to be as thorough as scientists in the way we use and understand the concepts.

The survival-strategy concept is one we will look at again with regard to maintenance; plants from similar habitats with a similar survival strategy tend to require a similar maintenance regime.

Learning from wild habitats

In the previous chapter we looked at how much contemporary planting practice is inspired by nature. Certain habitats inspire planting styles more than others do. To some extent this is because of practical and functional considerations: shallow artificial soils in urban environments approximate to the conditions available to plants growing on limestone, so an interest in dry meadows as ornamental habitats is entirely rational. Fashion and romanticism, however, drive society's interest in particular styles, and unfortunately neither is a very good guide to actually making things work in practice or to a precise and meaningful discussion of planting options in gardens and landscapes. *Meadow* and *prairie*, for example, are two terms which are often used in the gardening media without any clear explanation of what they mean – which is very confusing for the gardening public.

Here we look at some of the most inspirational wild habitats, how they are influencing contemporary planting design, and how they might do so in the future.

▲ Meadows have inspired much contemporary planting design, but it is important to recognize that most herbaceous planting, however wild-looking, is not strictly meadow, which is a habitat with a matrix of grass. These plantings at the Royal Horticultural Society's garden at Wisley are in a horticultural and ecological sense borders rather than meadows, but their aesthetic is very different from that of the conventional border.

• *Meadow*

As we have seen, meadow is semi-natural grassland which is cut during the summer months for a hay crop as part of traditional agricultural practice. In much of lowland Europe it has been replaced by other systems (arable, pasture and grass silage) and has largely disappeared, or it has been 'improved' by overseeding with ryegrass and high-nitrogen fertilizers. This loss has meant a considerable reduction in both biodiversity and visual richness in the landscape, since much traditional meadow had a huge, and very beautiful, range of wildflower and grass species. Not surprisingly, meadow as a concept has become part of the romantic view of traditional countryside which is held by many consumers in western Europe, and which the purveyors of 'organic' and 'natural' products are only too keen to promote. The re-creation of meadow in gardens can be seen as part of this romanticism. Furthermore, meadow is used to describe any contemporary naturalistic perennial-based planting – an inaccurate usage which can cause great confusion.

As many have discovered, making meadows is actually extremely difficult, because of the tendency of vigorous grasses to swamp slower-growing wildflowers. It is much easier to make meadows on low-fertility soils, particularly calcareous ones; it is not impossible on more fertile ones – but serious dedication is required. In terms of

aesthetics, meadows are arguably of limited value to many gardeners and landscape designers, as their flowering season is relatively short – early summer and little more, at least if only north European wildflower species are used. As a response to this, some people working in the field of garden and landscape design have tried to develop artificial meadow habitats, using a range of non-native herbaceous plants in grass, with a once- or twice-a-year mowing regime. In his work at Sheffield University James Hitchmough is carrying out scientific documentation of this. For maritime climates with a long growing season, the results are not particularly encouraging: the grasses have an inbuilt advantage over perennials, as they can grow almost year-round, whereas the vast majority of herbaceous plants are handicapped by having a dormant season. Exceptions are a few flowering perennials which also have a long growing season – many geranium species, in particular. Those perennials with large leaves which shade out surrounding grasses over a long season can also be successful – vigorous symphytum, kniphofia and echinops species are examples. In more continental climates, the possibilities for what might be called 'perennial meadow' are almost certainly greater. Here the results of the researchers at Hochschule Wädenswil in Switzerland promise to be something to watch.

Another possibility for an ornamental version of the meadow is where tussock-forming ornamental grasses are used to create a matrix which visually dominates, with flowering perennials inserted as a minority element. Piet Oudolf's use at one project in England (Bury Court in Hampshire) of a solid mass of *Deschampsia cespitosa* with a few *Trifolium rubens* poking through is an example which has been copied now by several other designers. There are no doubt possibilities for using a variety of other short- to medium-height tussock-forming grasses in this way. We would stress 'tussock-forming' grasses, because grasses which run to form turf or sod – that is, those which form the basis of true meadow and pasture – are too aggressive to combine with many flowering perennials, as well as being generally less ornamental. Unlike true meadows, which are mown using heavy-duty mowing equipment, these plantings would have to be maintained in the same way as conventional herbaceous plantings – with weeds controlled and plants cut back by less mechanized and more laborious methods.

• *Dry meadow, steppe and short-grass prairie*
The richest and most visually exciting meadow floras are those of thin calcareous soils, where the growth of competitive grasses is limited and the opportunities for lower, more stress-tolerant and slower-growing grasses and wildflowers are consequently greater. In central Europe in particular, the flora of this habitat is often strikingly beautiful, particularly in early summer, with a myriad of wildflowers flowering amid short turf. Further east the dry meadow grades into steppe, a habitat which is halfway to semi-desert. Steppe, too, can have remarkably high levels of biodiversity (a rate of 80 flowering plant species per square metre has been reported in Ukraine).

Dry meadow and steppe habitats have inspired some of the most beautiful plantings in Germany, for example in the Westpark in Munich, where drought-tolerant perennials and bulbs are brought together for a spectacular early-summer flowering season, with bearded iris hybrids (whose ancestors originated in this habitat) playing a

43

▲ Short-grass prairie is a habitat made up of tussocky grasses, and is typical of drier areas of the American Midwest. It is analogous to the steppe of eastern Europe and central Asia. Not surprisingly it is very drought-tolerant. A variety of flowering herbaceous species grows between the tussocks, leaving behind distinctive seedheads for the winter months.

particularly prominent role. Later in the summer and autumn, and indeed in the winter too, grasses and the grey-silver hummocks of sub-shrubs such as lavenders dominate. The 'Silbersommer' plantings (see page 31) are also inspired by these habitats.

Such plantings thrive on sites which experience seasonal drought much better than most perennials, and in years where there is some summer rainfall, pioneer species with their long flowering seasons can give particularly good results, the crimson buttons of *Knautia macedonica* being particularly good value. The fact that some species are evergreen or have good winter structure (such as durable seedheads) is a great advantage for this type of planting.

In North America the most obvious equivalent is the short-grass prairie of the Great Plains, a habitat with a great many attractive grasses and a huge variety of wildflowers. Other North American habitats which could offer inspiration for situations with shallow alkaline soil or seasonal drought include the Alvar of the Great Lakes region where there is very thin soil overlaying limestone, the granite-rock flora of the southern Appalachians, where a variety of plants survive not just thin soil but an impervious rock beneath, and the tussock-grass floras of the West, now very degraded by the invasion of sod-forming grasses of European-origin.

With so many urban soils being shallow and full of calcareous rubble, the potential for using plantings inspired by these habitats is considerable. Green roofs, or other situations where there is a shallow (and hence drought-prone) artificial soil layer, are also ideal locations.

There are two main provisos regarding these drought-tolerant plantings, one for regions where there is year-round rainfall and one for those where there is not. In regions where the depth and/or character of the soil rather than low rainfall is the limiting factor on what can be grown, there is the problem posed by invasive weed species. In regions with a dry summer climate these are only infrequently a problem as they do not survive drought in the way that the desired plants do, but in more humid climates, the drought-tolerant vegetation, which is often quite widely spaced, can be invaded by weeds, especially in summers with higher than average rainfall. These

◄ For many German planting designers, the steppe communities of dry soils in central and eastern Europe have been a major inspiration. They include a very wide range of species with a tolerance of dry and difficult sites, making them useful for many urban and post-industrial locations. This is at the Hermannshof garden, Weinheim.

plantings can then become relatively high-maintenance. This is certainly the case in the Munich Westpark, where the climate is clearly not dry enough to restrict the growth of a variety of weeds and maintenance is consequently an issue.

In climates where this type of vegetation is the norm, there is the possibility of non-regionally native species becoming invasive. Dry meadow, and steppe vegetation even more so, has an open character and it appears to be more vulnerable to infiltration by aggressive exotics; in the west of the United States, the sod-forming festuca and other European grasses have done enormous damage to native floras, fundamentally changing their character, while in central and eastern Europe several American tree and shrub species, notably *Robinia pseudoacacia* and *Amorpha canescens* have started to colonize dry meadow habitats. It might be advisable for people making these plantings to stick to species from their own continent, at least in locations outside urban areas.

• Tall-grass prairie

The tall-grass prairie flora of the North American Midwest is extraordinary for its rich and diverse flora. Once covering vast areas of the continent with a sea of tall, waving grasses and perennials, it has been reduced to a tiny fraction of its former extent, largely by agriculture. Over the last few years, however, the restoration of prairie, or its

► Even in moist maritime climates like that of England there are dry situations. This planting designed by Noel Kingsbury for thin soil on a sloping site uses a combination of hardy, drought-tolerant species from steppe, dry-meadow and Mediterranean-zone habitats.

45

▼ Prairie plants also have considerable biodiversity value, plus autumn and winter interest – for example the showy seedheads of *Asclepias speciosa*.

▲ Tall grass prairie in autumn with the grass *Andropogon gerardii* dominating, with *Eryngium yuccifolium* and on the right, the seedheads of a *Helianthus* species.

use as a landscape element, has become one of the fastest-growing aspects of natural landscape practice in North America. It has also attracted great interest in Europe.

Natural prairie, like meadow, consists mostly of grasses, with a minority element (around 25 per cent) of flowering herbaceous perennials or *forbs*. Growing from ground-level resting buds in spring, it can reach to well over human head height by late summer, its speed of growth fuelled by the intensity of the growing season – short but hot and humid. Although there are some species which flower in early summer, the vast majority of prairie grasses and perennials flower late – classic behaviour for competitive-type plants. Once winter has set in, many prairie species continue to form an imposing sight, at least for a few months, since their stiff stems stand blustery weather well and their seedheads can be impressive in frost and snow. So, it is not surprising that many prairie plants have been introduced into horticulture – many of our favourite late-summer and autumn perennials originate in prairie or other similar North American habitats.

In the United States and Canada it is customary to sow prairie as a seed mix, composed of grasses and perennials in the approximate 3:1 ratio found in the wild. It is possible to get prairie mixes for a variety of different habitats, as well as with a variety of different aesthetic criteria, primarily height and colour. In Europe, 'prairie' has taken on a wider meaning, being used by some to describe any naturalistic planting involving tall perennials whatever their origin. 'Real' prairie seed sowings involving grasses are not particularly successful in Europe, as some of the grasses do not germinate well, nor do they flourish particularly as adults in the cooler summers. Instead, mixes comprising the flowering perennial elements only have been used, albeit on a small scale so far, with much valuable research being done by James Hitchmough in Sheffield. Cassian Schmidt's planted combinations of prairie perennial and other compatible species at Hermannshof have successfully demonstrated how striking they can be for medium- to large-scale plantings in public spaces.

Prairie-style planting is attracting a lot of attention in Europe because it appears to solve a problem – that of high soil fertility which, as we have seen, renders it very difficult to establish attractive and diverse native-plant communities. Prairie appears to offer the possibility of low-maintenance planting with a long season of interest for human users and is a valuable resource for wildlife – the flowers attract huge numbers of butterflies and usually provide a good seed crop for birds. Unlike the far less vigorous European wildflowers, prairie plants are able to sustain a high level of diversity on fertile soils, even though there is a lot of inter-species competition. If grown at a high density, they seem to be able to resist weed incursions too.

However, it is early days. It is difficult to know how prairie plantings will survive long-term, whether their diversity will remain or whether a few species may overcome the others, or whether they will survive the depredations of the snails and slugs which flourish in a climate where the winters are considerably less severe than in North America, to say nothing of the aggressive European weed flora. Even if the plantings last only between five and ten years though, they may well be seen as a cost-effective treatment for public spaces.

► *Molopospermum peloponnesiacum* is a large
umbellifer from woodland edge habitats in the Balkans.
Tall-herb communities include many large and imposing
umbellifers. Most are biennial, but this is, usually,
longer-lived.

49

▼ Digitalis are woodland-edge plants, and often form part of tall-herb communities. Nearly all are biennial or short-lived perennials, but self-sow extensively. This is the very elegantly narrow *Digitalis ferruginea*, which looks particularly fine *en masse*.

► *Aconitum* is a very important tall-herb genus, with a great many showy species across Eurasia. This is *A. napellus*, a common early summer-flowering plant from Europe. Some more recently introduced ones from the Far East usefully flower later.

• *Tall-herb flora*

Among the most luxuriant floras of all in cool temperate climates are what are called 'tall-herb' communities. These flourish in areas of fertile moist soil, usually in the light shade of woodland or some tree cover. They are more frequent in mountain areas, where streams bringing high levels of nutrients from rapid erosion flow through valleys. The growth of grasses is often limited by either shade or gradient, so allowing the plant community to be dominated by broad-leaved perennials. In North America there is a clear connection to the prairie, with many species of aster, eupatorium, solidago and others. In Europe and Asia, the tall-herb flora is arguably more distinct, species of filipendula, persicaria, ligularia and aconitum being among the most distinctive.

Tall-herb flora is not as well known or understood as many other plant communities. It deserves more attention for the undoubted drama of many of its plants and for its relative shade tolerance, but also because of its ability to compete on fertile soils. Certain species of physostegia and lysimachia are good examples, showing a tendency to form solid monocultural weed-suppressing stands that can be very useful in public places and other large-scale plantings. Their lush growth does not make for good structural strength, however, and they tend to offer less winter interest than prairie plants. One reason for the relative, and rather regrettable, lack of interest in tall-herb communities is perhaps to do with access. They can only rarely be appreciated by the side of the road, usually requiring a good hike into the mountains to find examples, and then they tend to be found in relatively small patches. They are not as spectacular as meadows and prairies – not so photogenic. In addition, some of the most interesting tall-herb floras are to be found in areas which are currently well off the beaten track and dangerous to visit owing to political and economic instability, notably the Caucasus and eastern Siberia.

51

▼ Species and hybrids of *Helleborus* are among the most valued woodland plants for spring interest. Here they are flowering among emerging clumps of a *Geranium* species and the shoots of a *Polygonatum*. Herbaceous interest in spring tends to be low-level and scattered, which makes the repetition of plants across space particularly important.

• *Woodland floor*

Well established as an inspirational habitat by Gertrude Jekyll and many others, the use of shade-loving plants to form a low-level tapestry in shaded areas is quite often seen in larger private gardens and some public spaces: bulbs and other geophytes such as spring-flowering anemones in combination with low-growing perennials and ferns. Woodland plants tend to flower early and many are evergreen or have distinctive and attractive foliage. While the majority tend to stay low, some additional height and structure can be introduced through the use of taller plants such as ferns and perennials such as east Asian anemones and cimicifugas (a genus now classed by botanists under *Actaea*).

Certain woodlanders are very effective at forming solid mats of growth. This has led to a rather debased version of this planting style whereby large mats of 'ground cover'

▲ The royal fern *Osmunda regalis* is one of the most imposing of temperate-climate ferns, forming clumps which are very long-lived. It makes a fine focal-point plant for moist soil plantings, but does better on acidic soils.

– *Hedera helix*, pachysandra, symphytum – are used to create a very low-maintenance but monotonous green surface. Certainly some species are very competitive and tend to eliminate each other over time, but there are possibilities for using less aggressive ones and developing a more complex planting. Where shade is only light, there is especially little excuse for the 'green cement' look, as a great many species will thrive, including quite a few pioneer species such as aquilegia, meconopsis and digitalis, which will constantly seed themselves around, creating an atmosphere of spontaneity.

• *Wetland*

Waterside sites and others with a high level of water throughout the year are home to a range of mostly luxuriant-looking plants, able to sustain their lush and expansive style of growth because of the high level of resources – water and nutrients. In contrast, low-nutrient and acidic conditions allow the development of only a very low and almost ascetic flora – peat bog. The latter is rarely appreciated for its subtle aesthetic value, the plantings in the parks of Amstelveen in the Netherlands being among the few where this is the case.

Wetland plantings tend to obey their own rules and be relatively resistant to the exertions of the designer. The plants are strong competitive-type growers and tend to fight it out for space – often resulting in a very low species count in smaller plantings. Dramatic large-scale plantings can be made with relatively few species as well.

There are very good reasons as to why a stricter 'natives-only' policy should be employed in any wetland environment which is connected to a natural river system. Some of the most invasive alien-species problems have occurred in wetland environments, even in regions such as north-west Europe where these problems have tended to be rare. Not only are most wetland plants extremely vigorous, but both seed and pieces of root can be spread downstream with great ease.

One field that might encourage a greater design interest in wetland planting is the new one of 'natural swimming pools', where plants are used to filter and cleanse water for swimming. Beds of wetland plants are used for an essentially functional reason, yet in a situation where aesthetics are very important. This is definitely an area to watch.

Planting in space

◄ A group of dynamic and colourful plants seen in relative close-up. How we see plants depends very much on our proximity to them. Here are grey *Eryngium giganteum*, blue *Salvia* x*superba* 'Mainacht' and *Achillea* 'Wesersandstein'.

Gardens and other planted areas inevitably have surroundings. Their relationship to these surroundings plays a crucial role in what the garden feels like; indeed, a large part of a garden's identity may derive from its surroundings. But the relationship can also work the other way, and gardens may have an impact on what surrounds them. Here we want to look at various aspects of the relationship between the garden and the wider landscape, and in particular at the relationship between planting and landscape. We then go on to look at the larger-scale elements in gardens that act as both framework and context for planting – lawns, borders and paths.

Planting and the wider landscape

Gardens can either embrace or deny their surroundings. Secret gardens expressly aim to cut themselves off from the outside world, but many urban gardens aim to do the same, to ensure seclusion and to create a sense of a private world. Gardens that do not try to isolate themselves inevitably have some relationship to what is around them; they cannot remain neutral, as the surroundings are inescapably part of the experience of being in these kinds of garden. Designers can choose to relate to surroundings at a number of different levels, perhaps best summarized by a gradient:

complete seclusion	separation	distraction	inclusion	borrowed landscape	involvement
the secret garden	establishing a clear boundary between the garden and the outside world, making a statement that what happens *inside* is distinct and *different*	making the garden design so strong and inward-looking that the viewer is rarely tempted to look beyond it	the garden relates to its surroundings in some way	the Japanese concept of actively bringing a landscape element into the garden, to make it an integral part of the garden's identity	the garden belongs to the landscape and tries to be part of it; indeed, it seeks to dissolve the boundaries

• In the *complete seclusion* of the secret or hidden garden, it is impossible to see the surroundings that lie beyond the garden boundary.
• Conventional front gardens are a good example of *separation*. They are for show – it is possible to see everything at once. Because the owner's identity is on display for everyone to see, the garden can make a statement about belonging to a community, or state a defiant desire to be different.
• The urban back garden is often a 'within' experience, personal, with scope for creativity and fantasy. If it does not aim at seclusion, it may aim for *distraction*, so that surroundings become unnoticed and almost irrelevant.
• Many country gardens aim at some level of *inclusion*, of belonging to their

▶ Drifts of *Allium hollandicum* 'Purple Sensation', *Phlomis tuberosa* and *Astrantia major* 'Roma' in the borders at Wisley emphasize the power of repetition. A background of trees and shrubs forms an effective framework for the planting, their green linking to the green of the foliage in the border and helping to provide a context.

57

▼ In regions where deciduous trees dominate the landscape, their use helps to link the planting location to the wider surroundings. In terms of 'visual ecology' it rarely matters whether they are native species or not. This is *Pyrus ussuriensis*.

surroundings. This can be quite low-level, such as just having a nice view over a backdrop of farmland, or it can be more active, where views are deliberately framed by hedges or other features in order to *borrow* selected landscape elements such as trees or hills.

• Country gardens which aim at real *involvement* try to blur the boundaries between the garden and their surroundings.

Visual ecology

Increasingly people are making gardens in landscapes where there was little gardening in the past, or where gardening had a strongly traditional character. These gardens, along with houses and other buildings, may often have a negative impact on the landscape, primarily because they stand out, but also because they can reduce any sense of regional distinctiveness. The neo-classical villas and vaguely Italianate gardens full of brilliant bougainvillaea and classical columns that sprawl across hillsides in many Mediterranean or other warm-climate zones are a good example. The impact that such houses and gardens have on landscapes is becoming of increasing concern to some designers: John Brookes is a designer and writer who has made his views on this very clear (Brookes, 1998).

So, if one is making a garden in a rural area, how is it possible to create something that has character and style but which also has a sense of belonging to its surroundings? The issue needs to be addressed from two directions – looking out and looking in.

The garden owners look out, and may or may not want their garden to look as if it is part of the landscape. More crucial, from the standpoint of other landscape users, is the view looking in – does the garden have a sense of belonging to the land or does it stand out? Gardens in areas of great natural beauty which can be seen from a long way away are clearly a considerable intrusion. Because of their size, trees play an important role in how a garden relates to its surroundings (also see pages 134-140).

Hedges and boundaries

Hedges are needed for a variety of reasons: purely functional – screening from the wind, keeping out the neighbour's grazing animals and so on, and symbolic – a boundary demarcating one's garden and property. Hedges isolate and separate, but because they make green and living boundaries, they are less abrupt than walls or solid fences. Similarly, a relatively informal hedge (one that is not clipped into a uniform geometric shape) is a less clear boundary than a formal one. If hedges are part of the local landscape, such as the hawthorn-based ones common in north-west Europe, then the use of one around the garden may act as more a bond with the surrounding cultural landscape than an intrusion. However a dark evergreen such as the notoriously fast-growing Leyland cypress (x*Cupressocyparis leylandii*) may be a good windbreak, but it forms an alien intrusion in many rural landscapes, and one which can be seen from a considerable distance.

59

▲ Even in regions where hedges are not a part of the cultural landscape, their popularity is growing, as they are a useful way of combining a variety of decorative shrubs with a specific purpose, and they can have considerable wildlife value. When clipped into interesting shapes, as at Hummelo, then their visual appeal is even greater.

Planting to blend in

A sensitive handling of the transition between garden and surrounding countryside can be achieved by using planting that – while ornamental – is similar enough to what might be seen in the surrounding landscape. In many gardens shrubs can play an important role here, especially at the boundaries, where they can serve both a screening function and a blurring of the garden/landscape distinction. Clearly this will be most effective if they are similar in form to those likely to be found in the surroundings.

Perennial planting, too, can play a part. The advantage of perennials is that because of their smaller size they impact less on their surroundings than woody plants – it is possible to have even quite exotic-looking species like kniphofias, as they will have minimal impact at distances over a hundred metres or yards. From within the garden, though, the choice of perennials can have a major impact on the relationship between surrounding countryside and the garden. Because of the way they tend to dominate most open habitats in temperate zones, grasses encourage us to read the garden as more 'natural' and can create a strong psychological linkage to the landscape. In much of Europe, umbellifers (members of the cow parsley / Queen Anne's lace family, Apiaceae) are also a large element in the landscape, so ornamental umbellifers such as species of selinum, angelica and peucedanum can also help to create a rustic feel. In North America, where the daisy family tends to dominate in late summer and autumn, species of aster, solidago and helianthus will help to make this link. In general, species with masses of small flowers are read as more natural by most people than large or brightly coloured flowers, and are more appropriate where links to rural landscape are wanted.

One way of making a link with the surroundings is to use some locally native species in garden plantings. This is an approach that is all too rarely used by garden designers, despite the growing popularity of all-native meadow and prairie plantings. Many locally native plants are ornamental enough to be included in garden plantings, although they will be welcomed only if they do not have an invasive habit.

► This path, at the Pensthorpe Wildfowl Park in Norfolk, leads the eye onwards and outwards into the surrounding landscape. The planting may be colourful and decorative, but its gentle shapes do not conflict with the landscape.

▼ Blue-mauve *Perovskia atriplicifolia*, pink *Liatris spicata* and the grass *Deschampsia cespitosa* form a striking combination in this Oehme–van Sweden planting and illustrate the more intermingled style that the practice is now developing. Its visually soft character renders it very suitable for rural locations, as well as urban.

▼▼ Grasses and umbellifers are the kind of low-key plants which can very effectively create psychological links to rural landscapes. Here fennel (*Foeniculum vulgare*) grows with *Deschampsia cespitosa*.

Taking a step further, one of the best ways of integrating a garden with rural surroundings is with meadows or other native-based plantings – they will be seen as more clearly belonging to the landscape than to the garden. Areas of lawn can be turned into meadow or allowed to grow long for at least part of the year.

A sense of scale

The impact that plantings make on the viewer is very much to do with the scale upon which they are created. Certain scale factors contribute positively to the impact of a planting:

- A planting that relates to the extent (or the apparent extent) of the whole area will have more impact.
- Large plants are more likely to create impact and enhance the apparent size of the area.
- Large masses of one species can enhance impact and increase the sense of scale.
- Repetition and rhythm enhances scale, as it suggests an awareness of the whole area over which the repetition is made.

Other factors give a planting a reduced sense of scale or impact:

- An insignificant planting in a large area, or one with a particularly dramatic backdrop.
- Small plants, especially if the planting area or the site is extensive.
- A lack of repetition.

Clearly, large areas need big, confident plantings. This applies particularly to public spaces. However, the cost of plants and of the maintenance required to keep them looking good may appear to rule this out. As an alternative, a more naturalistic planting may be considered – one that needs lower maintenance. Wilder-style plantings also tend to look good, or at least respectable, with lower levels of maintenance. In very

61

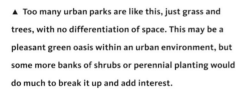

▲ Too many urban parks are like this, just grass and trees, with no differentiation of space. This may be a pleasant green oasis within an urban environment, but some more banks of shrubs or perennial planting would do much to break it up and add interest.

Urban landscapes can overwhelm unless they are counterposed with substantial areas of green. The detail of this planting is also an effective way of providing contrast to the buildings, as it 'detains the eye' and so rivals the background for the mind's attention. Planting by Piet Oudolf within a framework designed by Gustafson Guthrie Nichol Ltd at the Lurie Garden in Chicago. ▲

large areas, meadow, prairie or other sown planting may be the most cost-effective way of creating and managing herbaceous plantings.

In urban areas, meadows and other wilder plantings may be well received, but as a rule urban dwellers often seem to prefer more managed plantings, or a form of nature which is more decorative than many of the native-based plantings which have become popular over recent years. The concept of 'enhanced nature' developed by Nigel Dunnett and James Hitchmough at Sheffield University is one way of addressing this problem – the use of robust, decorative, non-native species in combination with low-maintenance natives. Brighter colours, a wider range of attractive species and a longer flowering season are all factors that are appreciated by onlookers and help give these more naturalistic and ecological plantings wider acceptability.

Both gardens and parks are spaces that can be made to seem larger by putting in more levels of experience – more things to look at, more levels of complexity to engage the eye. At its simplest, a meadow looks larger than mown grass, and a garden with borders, shrubs and hedges looks larger than a meadow. As complexity increases, so does the level of attention and engagement needed to comprehend it, and so it seems larger. But at the same time there is an apparently paradoxical need to make urban parks more intimate in character. Large spaces of mown grass punctuated only by the odd tree are all too easily dominated by a few people, especially if they are playing a noisy game of football. Such spaces need differentiating to create more intimate areas that feel separate from the whole, allowing multiple activities to take place – but not *too* separate, and certainly not secluded, as urban dwellers inevitably feel threatened by enclosing vegetation. Shrubs may be very useful for screening and creating intimacy and creating a more gardened feeling, but public perceptions of them is that they can shelter anti-social elements: beds of lower groups of robust perennials can offer a definite advantage here. This need for intimacy in public areas is not in fact a paradox, as improved differentiation encourages more people to use public space, effectively making it bigger.

Very simple means can be used to make monotonous areas of lawn look larger as well as creating more interest. Bands or strips of planting, even if planted as a monoculture, serve to break up space, creating the illusion of greater extent through increasing the level of interest and therefore the amount of engagement the brain needs. Trees or shrubs can also do the same, but only if they are used in such a way that their foliage does not conceal from view substantial areas of grass.

Scale is an issue of particular importance in small gardens, generally urban ones, where there is little in the way of views out and where the surroundings may be unattractive and even oppressive. Tall plants in a small space create an impression of depth, and if the boundaries are concealed, then the sense of restriction which often exists in urban gardens can be dispelled. Such bold strategies avoid the trap of triviality that all too often leads to fussiness: in the words of James van Sweden, 'small plants in a small garden make it feel smaller'.

▼ At Scampston Hall, the grass *Molinia caerulea* 'Poul Petersen' is used *en masse* in 'rivers', an idea developed from Piet Oudolf's salvia stream at the 'Dreampark' in Enköping, Sweden. The molinia has a long season of interest, from May to January, and can be combined with bulbs such as crocus, galanthus and narcissus.

► Once divided by these *Molinia* rivers, the lawn area appears larger than plain grass and is turned into a more dynamic space.

▲ This area of lawn at Scampston Hall has been broken up by using blocks of box. The overall effect is still a green and visually simple counterpoint to colourful borders, but the effect is novel, so creating a very contemporary impression.

The context of planting

• *Lawns*

Traditional European garden practice has tended to make the lawn the most visually dominant element. In so many domestic gardens it occupies a large central space, giving the impression that any other elements – borders of perennials or banks of shrubs – are pushed outwards to the edges or flung there by a kind of centrifugal force. Lawn allows access to plantings, which may be an advantage, but sometimes the designer may also wish to allow people to see only from a distance. This is an advantage of an expanse of water, as it makes it impossible for onlookers to get any closer than the designer intends them to, effectively increasing the impact of a distant planting.

As European garden style influenced the development of gardens in other countries, it was perhaps inevitable that the lawn would become central to gardens around the world. This international spread has come at a great cost, though, as people try to make a garden feature that is perfect for the cool, moist weather of north-west Europe

▲ There is still plenty of lawn at Bury Court in Hampshire, but rather than dominating it flows between expansive beds of perennials, a stylized grass meadow, and blocks of clipped shrubs.

work in completely different climates. The lawn has also been taken to extremes, as in the United States, where vast expanses of mown lawn can be seen in many suburban neighbourhoods, almost at the expense of anything else. Adding up the environmental costs of all this grass is an alarming exercise: the fuel used to power lawnmowers, their emissions, the fertilizers, herbicides and pesticides applied to keep them in perfect condition, and the enormous amount of irrigation to keep them green.

We would add our voices to the growing chorus of those who want to rethink the lawn and challenge its supremacy in the garden. We think we should ask: 'do you want to be a groundsman or a gardener?' Lawns in their place, and in regions where they grow verdant for most of the year, can be beautiful; we do not want to get rid of them, but only to question the importance they have in so many garden cultures. It is interesting and encouraging to see the variety of challenges to the lawn that are now emerging throughout the world, many of which involve perennials. In the United States Wolfgang Oehme and James van Sweden have brought together great masses of grasses and perennials to evoke prairie and wild grassland, using conventional mown grass as narrower areas of contrast and as access routes. Their style is very much an artistic version of the prairie style that is gaining ground in the American Midwest, where gardeners are increasingly replacing lawn grass, so difficult to manage in the heat of the summer, with combinations of wild prairie grasses and wildflowers. In Germany the mass planting of perennials in parks is explored through narrow paths, with areas of lawn quite physically separate. To someone on a path within the perennial plantings, the plants can become all-encompassing, but the viewer standing outside the plantings, on the lawn, sees another aspect – a distinct fringe of growth which becomes progressively denser through the year as the herbaceous plants grow.

We would propose what is sometimes seen in dry climates: large beds of planting, with smaller, more 'thought-out' zones of grass. Instead of using lawn grass as a matrix, use it for a purpose, so that it flows between areas planted with perennials, ornamental grasses, ground-covering plants, shrubs or native plants.

• *Borders*
Although we wish to encourage people to rethink radically how we use perennials – that is, to discover ways of growing them other than in conventional linear borders – we recognize that the border is a format that will remain popular. Apart from anything else, it fits in well with the layout of so many gardens and parks. Particularly where the basic layout is a historic one, there may be little opportunity to change this fact. But we think that border plantings can often be made more exciting.

When walking along a traditional border, especially a long one, the viewer is part of a linear process, something that has a beginning, a middle and an end – it can almost be seen as having a narrative. Gertrude Jekyll realized this and organized the colours in her borders in bands that formed a progression, each stage preparing the eye for the next. Nori and Sandra Pope have worked with colour in a similar way at Hadspen House in Somerset, in particular creating a spectrum effect in a long curving border that runs along a south-facing wall, with plants of related colours grouped, and with each group gradually blending in to the next. They often use the language of music to

67

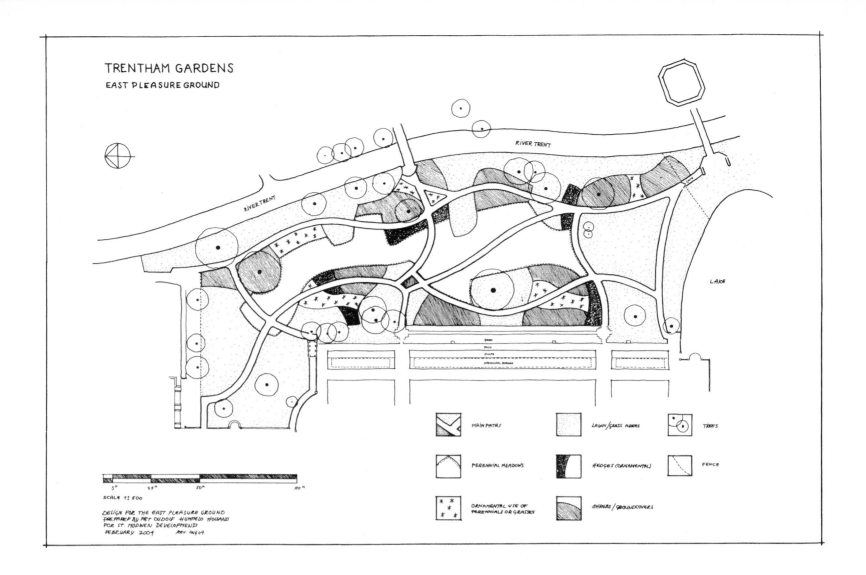

TRENTHAM GARDENS
EAST PLEASURE GROUND

RIVER TRENT

RIVER TRENT

LAKE

MAIN PATHS   LAWN/GRASS AREAS   TREES

PERENNIAL MEADOWS   HEDGES (ORNAMENTAL)   FENCE

ORNAMENTAL USE OF PERENNIALS OR GRASSES   SHRUBS/GROUNDCOVERS

SCALE 1:500

DESIGN FOR THE EAST PLEASURE GROUND
PREPARED BY PIET OUDOLF HUMMELO HOLLAND
FOR ST MODWEN DEVELOPMENTS
FEBRUARY 2004   REV. 04509

▲ At Trentham, a park area developed within a nineteenth-century landscape, Piet Oudolf has changed the traditional role of the lawn so it is no longer the centrepiece or foreground. Instead, the perennial plantings have become the matrix, and within them are areas of monoculture, of grasses such as *Molinia*, *Sesleria* and *Panicum* or perennials like *Echinacea purpurea*. In spring there are plantings of bulbs, hellebores, *Anemone nemorosa* and others. Areas of lawn are embedded in the perennial mass. Paths between the different areas do the connecting, not the lawn.

describe what they do, comparing borders with symphonies, for example – a comparison which strongly emphasizes their linearity and sense of progression.

A border that you walk *along* is an ideal place in which to explore rhythm. Plants with distinctive form over a long season, especially with a strong vertical element or bold foliage, are particularly useful for this. A strong rhythm is another way of providing structure and coherence to a planting.

Much contemporary design uses plantings which radically extend the border, so that it is no longer linear and no longer clings to the boundaries of gardens or forms a mere backdrop. Rather than being something that one walks *along*, it is something one can plunge *into*. Using perennial planting in large masses with paths running between and through them creates a very different perspective for the visitor from the conventional situation where borders are something one looks at from the outside. This experience offers a journey through the planting that is more akin to walking through meadow or a prairie, with changing angles and distances allowing us to enjoy the plants in different ways. In the traditional 'English' border the onlooker looks *at* them 'like an army on parade', in the words of Prof. Peter Kiermeyer, the director of the Weihenstephan Institute in Germany, home of one of the world's largest collections of perennials. The origins of this probably lie in gardens of the Victorian and Edwardian eras, where a regiment of gardeners laboured to produce grand displays of plants for the enjoyment

◄ ▲ At Hummelo, Piet and Anja Oudolf's own garden in the eastern Netherlands , the repetition of yew as a structural theme plant creates a sense of visual unity. This gives the designer flexibility and the opportunity to do a variety of widely different things – to include a lot of plant varieties, varying colours, forms, patterns and so on in between. The rhythmical elements provide a 'macro' level of interest; the others form a more complex level of interest at the 'micro' level.

A variety of climbers, including *Wisteria* and *Celastrus* trained on to supports, creates structural interest at the end of the nursery area. ►►

69

▼ Piet Oudolf's perennial borders at the Royal Horticultural Society garden at Wisley have an enormous level of complexity – a vast range of plants combined in different ways, but all included within the same-sized planting strips, like a variety of different melodies contained by a continuous rhythm.

▲ Plantings in the Altlorenscheuerhof garden in Luxemburg are very expansive, dominating the garden, with areas of lawn flowing between the borders. Yet in some ways, the borders are still traditional, with taller plants in the centre of the border and to appreciate them the visitor still has to walk alongside the outer edge of the planting. There is more opportunity to see *over* the plantings than in traditional borders, however.

of the owners and their guests. Although these guests might wander around specifically to admire the plants, the garden was also a backdrop to an endless round of social and also political activity, as the grandees who owned the big gardens also dominated all levels of government. Borders were then, to some extent, glorified wallpaper. They also had to be as near perfect as possible, which meant that they could only be seen from a limited range of angles. Shorter plants hid the bare stems of taller ones, many of which were supported by hidden stakes.

Our attitude to plants now is very different, or at least it covers a wider range of attitudes. Planting is still a backdrop for many, but we also have a greater enjoyment of plants for their own sakes. We are certainly far less interested in absolute perfection. Plantings that treat perennials as the matrix of the garden or which offer a variety of ways of experiencing them offer us a range of angles and options. In particular when people are encouraged to walk *through* there is an invitation to an intimate involvement with the planting, the opportunity for a more deeply emotional experience; the plants look taller, possibly even overwhelming, and perhaps our journey is longer, as we stop more often and look more closely. Such a journey can be seen as therapeutic, a walking meditation among a stylized and artistically rendered version of nature.

For those interested in seeing how plants really grow, there is the possibility of examining their habit at close quarters. There is also the opportunity to see and get close to the range of insect and other life that lives among garden plants – we are now far more likely than in the past to see the garden as wildlife habitat and to be interested in the creatures that come to make it their home. Above all, given that for many urban people the garden (or the park) is the most important part of their experience of the natural world, encouraging people to walk through plantings is at root about helping them to get closer to nature.

► *Molinia caerulea* subsp. *arundinacea* 'Transparent' is a splendid focal point for autumn and early winter interest. Ornamental grasses such as this are now an important part of many herbaceous plantings, as they are recognized for their long season of interest and ability to evoke natural habitats.

• Paths and ways of looking

Now that the lawn is no longer the centrepiece of the garden, we need to rethink how we move across and explore the garden. In gardens where the lawn is reduced, lawn becomes more like a broad path, a river of green between shrub- or perennial-dominated masses. We are proposing a further development – that when the lawn shrinks to discrete areas rather than providing connections or access, there is a need for paths to provide access and to provide 'connective tissue' between the different, and possibly quite disparate, parts of the garden.

Entrances, both to parks and gardens, and to smaller areas within these spaces, play a crucial role in setting the scene. What confronts the visitor in the first few seconds of their stepping over the threshold? Is it something dramatic that immediately seizes their imagination, demanding their attention, making them walk over and look at it in greater detail, or is it something more subtle – a view over a variety of plantings, paths and features, which offer a variety of options. Designers have to decide how strongly they want to direct their public, and in particular how much they want to reveal at once. It is a fundamental rule of garden and landscape design that not everything

Paths *through* herbaceous plantings offer a very different experience to the traditional walking *past* a border. They are an opportunity to feel part of something rather than looking at it from outside.

▼ *Echinops, Helenium, Lythrum* and *Monarda* are the most striking elements of this 'walk-through' border.

◄ Here at Altlorenscheuerhof *Astilbe, Sesleria, Aster,*
Sedum, Helenium, Lythrum and *Persicaria* cultivars line
a path in midsummer.

should be visible immediately, as otherwise there is no stimulus to explore. But, working with living material, this is not something which it is possible to fix absolutely; there is both seasonal change and long-term change which can affect how much the visitor sees. Over the years, of course, trees, shrubs and bamboos which are used to control space grow, limiting the eye's access to the site. Such long-term growth needs to be considered at the design stage.

The perspective one has from paths varies greatly from season to season. Early in the year there is plenty of opportunity to look *over* plantings, as there will be no tall perennials, only whatever shrubs are used – spring-flowering perennials and bulbs are inevitably low-growing. There is often a sense of openness at this time of year and it is possible to look across the garden and see almost everything at once. As a consequence, it is often possible to create a strong sense of rhythm, by repeating certain plants or plant combinations – it is especially easy to do this with bulbs. By early summer, there will be a lot at knee-height, and some perennials will be taller; the view ahead around paths that run through perennial plantings will be reduced and there will be more of a sense of discovery. In late summer and autumn, if perennials that grow to head-height

▼ At Scampston Hall, people are not allowed into the centre of the garden right away but rather forced to walk along 'plantsman's walk' first, before entering the main area of the garden. There is delayed gratification, enhanced expectation. They are then brought out into the centre of the garden on the main axis. This makes the garden like a performance artwork.

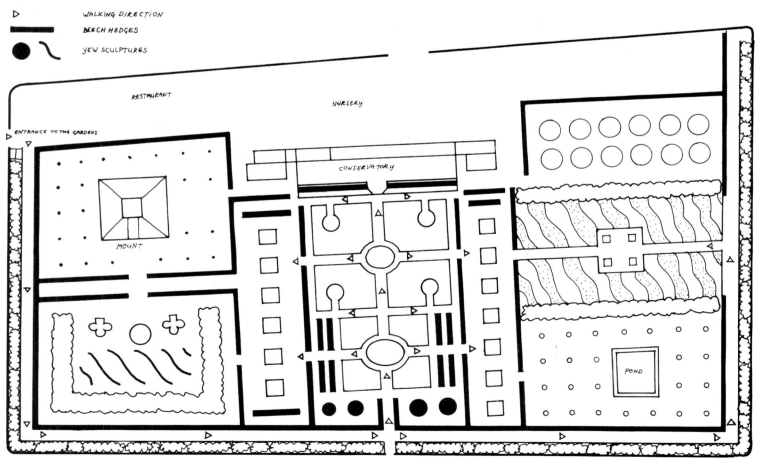

THE WALLED GARDEN AT SCAMPSTON HALL

or above are used, there is the sensation of walking among giants, of being dwarfed by vegetation, of being in a labyrinth. Whether one enjoys this is a matter of opinion: we love it, but we know that some people find it intimidating.

In the magnificent perennial plantings that can be seen in many German parks, paths play a crucial role in encouraging visitors to explore. The broad paths that connect one place to another are the ones that the majority of park users walk along. But there is often another series of narrower paths that set off into the planted areas, winding this way and that. The trick performed by their winding course is that it makes it difficult to see where they lead (or even that they exist) for more than a few paces forwards or backwards – the paths disappear behind vegetation. The illusion is thus created that the planting is a solid mass, with something of the feeling that one is in a wildflower meadow and, above all, *that there are no other paths* in this dream-like version of nature. In actual fact, it may be that there is nowhere in the planting that is more than three metres or yards from a path, which of course is necessary for maintenance purposes.

▲ Plantings at Hermannshof are very much in the 'open border' style, where visitors wander around on paths, coming very close to the plants, and looking over them to other areas of the garden. Many plant shapes, uprights in particular, are best appreciated this way.

This is the North American border, with a variety of *Helenium* and *Silphium* species and cultivars. ▶ ▶

81

Even in domestic gardens it is possible to achieve this result if paths are sufficiently narrow and winding.

One of the joys of having a system of paths like this is that round every corner there is a new experience, or at least the opportunity to create one. In smaller gardens this can play a crucial role in providing the sense of mystery and discovery that might otherwise be difficult to achieve. A system of circuits, in particular, appeals to many people, as these routes organize one's experience of the garden, and minimize the possibility of 'missing something'.

In gardens or parks where there is public access, the width of paths is important, and needs to be related to the level of foot traffic expected: a minimum of 1.2–1.8 m (4–6 ft) gives people enough space to pass each other without risking stepping into the border. Paths narrower than this must be very clearly given a special status, so that it is apparent that you enter them almost 'by invitation only'. Watching people move around shows that this hierarchy works well; the vast majority of casual visitors, who want to use the park plantings as a location for social interaction, use only the main paths, whereas those who are interested in plants and wildlife or who want to be alone are those who will make the extra effort to take the narrower paths.

Putting plants on show

Modern ways of displaying and combining plants are very different from traditional ways. Historically, plants were treated in gardens rather as art was produced – plants were treated either as artistic material or as art objects. Those who clipped evergreens into geometric forms and made topiary were treating plants as material much as a conventional sculptor would use stone or bronze. Other plants, mostly grown for their flowers, would be treated as objects to be displayed and appreciated for their individual beauty and value. This can be seen most clearly in seventeenth-century gardens, where intricate patterns of formal hedges define beds with precisely positioned plants separated by stretches of bare earth. Later in garden history, plants were treated in a less precious way, but the element of display and separation were still there; the late nineteenth-century herbaceous border created a luxuriant mass of flower, but each variety was placed precisely so that it would be displayed to perfection.

Developments in the art world have broken down old categories and divisions; new means of expression – installations, concept art and video – have challenged our very conception of what art is. Something similar has happened in garden design. For example, some modern plantings, such as wildflower meadows, can be read by onlookers almost not as gardens at all. A key difference is that plants are no longer treated as individual objects, but instead brought together as parts of a whole. It is the ways in which these parts are combined to make a meaningful and harmonious result that form the subject of this chapter.

Putting plants together

The bringing together or juxtaposing of plants is the issue at the heart of effective planting design. It is useful to consider a number of broadly defined approaches here before we launch into more detailed discussions.

COMBINING NEIGHBOURS | The traditional way of looking at plant combinations involves putting together plants that are highly effective next to one another. Some designers try to create entire plantings where each plant is located next to neighbours on the basis of a high level of visual interest, and particularly contrast, between them. This style is typical of the work of some of the classic English planting designers, such as Rosemary Verey and Christopher Lloyd. It can be very effective on a small scale, but can be visually exhausting on a larger one, particularly if there is a continual stress on contrast rather than harmony, as with the latter's work.

COMBINING FOR OVERALL EFFECT | In this approach the emphasis is much more on the appearance of the whole than on exact relationships between neighbouring plants. There may be a strong emphasis on overall harmony, as with the colour-focused work of Nori and Sandra Pope at Hadspen House in Somerset, or an emphasis on mild contrasts between clearly articulated forms, as in work by Oehme and van Sweden. It is less crucial for neighbouring plants to combine effectively than for *all* the species used to work well together, perhaps with some particularly arresting juxtapositions as

▼ *Echinacea purpurea* and *Selinum wallichianum* form
an attractive combination for mid- or late summer.
Its effectiveness is due as much to contrast in form as
to colour, but such combinations need good positioning
to be seen at their best.

► Juxtaposition of plant varieties can be very
effective, but can also be somewhat rigid and severe.
Here are blocks of *Helenium* 'Rubinzwerg' with
Sedum telephium 'Matrona'.

▲ It is the overall effect of this planting combination
(*Echinacea tennesseensis* with *Allium* 'Summer Beauty')
which creates the impact it does, the details of the
individual flowers blurring in the mind's eye.

▼ *Allium cristophii* and *Astrantia major* 'Roma' are
here combined so that they are intermingled, creating
a blurred tapestry effect from afar and the chance to
appreciate two species together close up.
This combination works because the colours harmonize,
and because of this the eye focuses more intently than
it usually does on the flower shapes. *Molinia caerulea*
subsp. *arundinacea* 'Transparent' is used for late
summer and autumn interest because this plant
develops later and is attractive until winter.

highlights. This approach is most appropriate for larger plantings where there is a
tendency for onlookers to view the whole rather than examine details.

INTERMINGLED COMBINATIONS | This relatively new approach seeks to do both –
to work on the 'macro' level to create plantings which are effective overall and on the
'micro' level to offer pleasure in detail. A relatively restricted number of plants is used,
and individuals or multiples of these are intermingled. This creates a block of planting
which is effective *en masse* as well as highlighting the visually striking juxtaposition of
individual plants.

Gardening with prepositions

How a garden or a planting is appreciated depends so on the viewpoint from which it is
seen: from above, from below, or from the same level. We can also talk about looking *at*
plantings, or *through* them, as well as *along* them and *over* them.

The angles at which plantings are viewed can be of crucial importance to their
visual effect – what may work in one place may not in another. Different aspects of
plants and of planting become visible when viewed from different positions.
Many grasses with attractive inflorescences and seedheads, for example, look at their
best when backlit or in silhouette and are unimpressive when looked down upon.
Consequently, when designing for a particular situation, the planting should reflect
what works best from the key viewpoints.

Gardens that are viewed from above may be seen from relatively close to if only a
gentle slope or small elevation is concerned, but if the main vantage point is much
higher up, then they will be need to be visible from much further away. A planting that
has been commissioned to be seen from, say, an office block or an elevated walkway
rather than at close quarters, will need to be boldly textured to make any impact.
Small plants will need to be placed in relatively large groups in order to have visual
impact. Plants with bold foliage will also be useful. A restriction in the number of
varieties used will also help to make a strong and coherent picture.

▲ The higher you stand, the more of the pattern of Piet Oudolf's borders at Wisley that you see. From the top the viewer looks *along* and *down* and can see the diagonals, while the long perspective gives the planting a meadow-like appearance. But turn around and look *up* the borders and the view is foreshortened, so the same planting works differently, with a much clearer view of the sequence of different layers and of the diversity of plants.

Gentle slopes, on the other hand, involve looking *across* and *over* the more distant areas, while the parts closer to the viewer are more likely to be looked *down on to*. In situations like this, common to many gardens, what you look at will change as it appears from different angles. What works well depends very much on the plants used, the site, and the tastes of the designer. There is much scope to experiment in combining a variety of plants and mixing them to create different effects. As a general rule, plants with more detail or subtle colouring will be appreciated best close up.

Taller plants, such as prairie or tall-herb woodland-edge species, also often look particularly effective on a gentle slope where the viewer looks *up* at them, which accentuates their size. These taller species can also be effective viewed from a distance of up to 15 m (50 ft) or so as a centrepiece to shorter surrounding planting. True prairie plants are so tall as to be best appreciated on horseback, which is why designers who work with prairie plantings have sometimes used decking to elevate the viewer. Meadow and prairie areas in a garden context can be appreciated not only by looking *over* them, but also from *within*, and the experience of viewing plantings from within is closely related to the discussion of how one is led through along a system of paths.

This may be a good place to reiterate the true meaning of 'meadow' as fields of grasses and wildflowers (the latter technically known as forbs – non-grassy perennials), which are cut at least once a year as part of a traditional agricultural regime. Meadows made up of a matrix of grasses, with a smaller proportion of wildflowers, are

increasingly popular in gardens. Whereas traditional borders are generally designed to be looked *at* and to some extent *along*, wildflower meadows are generally best appreciated by being *in* them, and since the plants are lower than eye level we look out *over* them – human head height is ideal for appreciating their drifts of intermingled colour and texture. We can see as individuals those flowers which are close to where we are standing, the remainder blurring into the kind of speckled drift that Monet conveyed so well in his paintings of poppyfields.

However, the meadow can serve as inspiration for what we might call a much more 'gardenesque' style of extensive herbaceous plantings designed to be managed as conventional borders rather than mown. The key to designing these *meadow-like* plantings is precisely that they are intended to be looked *over*, which is a very good way of appreciating shorter plants repeated in subtle semi-random patterns. If robust, low-maintenance species are used, such plantings can be very extensive, making them useful for public spaces. Small differences in the height of the plants used will be an important contribution to the overall visual texture. Grasses and perennials with tall, airy flower-heads and seedheads are often an important part of such plantings.

Complexity and diversity

One of the most important differences between natural and artificial plantings is their degree of complexity. In nature, herbaceous vegetation not only has far more individual plants per unit area, but also many more species – wildflower-meadow habitats can exceed 50 species per square metre or yard. Individual plants are also intimately interwoven, resulting in a tapestry of extraordinary complexity. In contrast, artificial plantings contain few species and individuals per unit area and tend to have very little

	Visual qualities and effects	Plants
DOWN ON	• bold shapes, large groups, pattern, individual plants in groups	• bold leaves, species that look good in groups, bright flowers, coloured foliage
OVER	• good for appreciating differences in height, repetition, rhythm and depth	• grasses, finely structured and flowering perennials, plants in drifts and groups of varying sizes, shorter plantings, hummock-forming sub-shrubs
UP AT	• good for backlighting, creates a feeling of being overwhelmed, emphasizes the size of large plants	• grasses, 'transparent' or open-structured perennials, bold foliage which can be backlit, taller perennials, bamboos with good canes
	• bold masses, tiered planting, textures	• taller perennials that need their lower parts hidden behind shorter ones, bright colours, bold and coloured foliage, ferns
THROUGH	• finely textured foliage, plantings with open structure	• 'transparent' perennials, taller perennials and grasses
ALONG	• plants that lean, rhythm and repetition of form and colour – especially for theme plants, sense of narrative	• bold leaves, grasses (for rhythm), blocks of colour

blending and intermingling. Generally they involve much lower levels of both complexity and diversity, and often they comprise large blocks of a single species – so-called monocultures.

Contemporary planting design is very much more concerned with biodiversity than planting ever was historically, a result of the growing awareness that artificial environments have been created at enormous ecological cost and that it is desirable to design landscapes that offer a place for wildlife as well as for humanity. It is now widely appreciated that horticultural plantings can offer an enormous range of opportunities for wildlife. As a general rule nature thrives on diversity, so the more plant species packed into a space, the more ecological niches there are and the higher the potential biodiversity. Natural processes tend strongly towards high levels of complexity, too. But, is complexity a good thing in design terms? At a time when many designers are working hard to make the planted landscape as wildlife-friendly as possible, this is an important question.

Complexity is one of the visual aspects of landscape that we value, but it is not the only one. Complexity can equal visual richness and therefore offer stimulation and excitement, but too much of it can be confusing and even disorientating – we need *coherence*, too. Coherence is about how easy something is to *read*, make sense of, find our way around. Only when a complex pattern is coherent can we actually enjoy complexity. As with all matters of aesthetics, however, perception of the balance of coherence and complexity is very subjective, and closely related to questions of cultural background, fashion and taste.

In planting schemes, the level of coherence and complexity is governed by a number of factors. One is simply the number of species or plant varieties: using fewer varieties generally makes a planting more coherent. Another is the size of the groups of plants used – ecologists talk about vegetation as being 'coarse-grained' or 'fine-

▲ Slopes provide an opportunity to look down on plantings or to look up at them. Looking down can generate a meadow-like effect. Here *Iris sibirica* flowers among a variety of other perennials in Noel Kingsbury's garden.

▲ Transparency is the effect whereby you can 'see through' plants with sparse foliage or stems to whatever is behind. It can be a particularly effective way of looking at blocks of colour. Here the grasses *Stipa gigantea* and *Miscanthus sinensis* 'Flamingo' provide the transparent element.

▼ *Persicaria amplexicaulis* is the foreground for a view over bold drifts of perennials at Pensthorpe in Norfolk. This angle allows colour and visual texture to be appreciated clearly.

▲ Seriously big perennials, late in the season, need to be looked up at. They can be an awe-inspiring sight. The tall purplish pink here is *Eupatorium purpureum* subsp. *maculatum* 'Atropurpureum'; the white is *Aster umbellatus*.

► Plantings past their main flowering season are often best seen by looking over them; subtle differences of colour and texture can be appreciated, particularly if some species are block-planted. *Astilbe* seedheads dominate the foreground.

▲ 'Windows' in hedges or fences are an invitation to look through, and get a 'sneak preview' of a planting or part of a garden. They can draw attention to particular features or vistas.

grained', the former referring to larger clumps of the same species, the latter to smaller ones, or simply intermingled individuals. There is yet another level, that of the relationship between the different groups – are there, for example, groups of groups? The size of plant groups also needs to be related to the size of the garden area.

• *Grouping or intermingling?*
A common practice throughout garden and landscape history has been the use of large blocks of the same species. However, in the hands of landscape architects with little training in plant usage, the block-planting approach has come to represent the nadir of planting design, epitomized by the blocks of shrubs around motorways and shopping malls that have made many of our urban environments so dull.

The intermingling of plants, as happens in natural vegetation, is rarely seen in gardens – it is almost as if designers and gardeners are somehow afraid of what will happen if plants are allowed to do this. Yet there are some very good reasons for experimenting with this approach. For gardens seeking to adopt a naturalistic aesthetic, it is one of the most obvious ways to create a feeling of naturalness. It is also a good way of establishing a sense of visual unity, as it makes it easier to scatter key plants around the garden and so establish a strong overall theme. Another reason is that it becomes possible to establish some very exciting combinations, bringing together colours, shapes and textures in an intimacy that cannot be achieved when they are grouped separately. Indeed, we would stress that intermingling can be used

for artistic effect in highly structured settings – it does not necessarily have to be part of a naturalistic approach.

A proviso, however, is that it is vital for those who design such intermingled combinations to have good horticultural knowledge, because the varieties brought together must have an identical maintenance regime and must be of similar competitiveness. Plantings with an intermingled style are also arguably more appropriate for public situations where the staff possess high skill levels.

The most complex plantings of all are meadow and prairie, where there are vastly more both of individual plants and of species per unit area than in any traditional horticultural situation. At this level of complexity the eye tends to read the plant mass as a whole, to see it as a dreamy plane, with little to focus on. This makes it extremely useful in the design of larger spaces. On the one hand such plantings can create a sense of romantic softness and lack of definition, and on the other these qualities can be used to counterpoint and indeed to highlight elements in the landscape which are focal points, such as built structures, trees or artworks. One of the best examples of this is the wildflower meadow at Christopher Lloyd's Great Dixter garden, where grass and wildflowers surround yew topiary.

Different environments clearly require different levels of complexity. For instance, commercial and roadside plantings tend to be seen by people who have no particular interest in plants, and in any case usually have little time to stand and admire. This is

▲ Intermingling contrasted with block planting can make for some dramatic effects. Here a mass of *Calamagrostis xacutiflora* 'Stricta' is a background for a blend of blue-mauve *Perovskia atriplicifolia*, a yellow *Coreopsis verticillata* cultivar and *Liatris spicata*. This is an Oehme–van Sweden Associates planting at the Chicago Botanic Garden.

▲ Intermingling varieties creates possibilities for a range of different effects. Here *Sanguisorba menziesii* grows alongside *Salvia* 'Serenade'. There is a gentle colour contrast but a similarity in flower-spike shape. These two plants tend to favour different environments, *Salvia* preferring dry soil and *Sanguisorba* requiring moisture; but this is not a problem in climates where drought is rare, as in garden conditions both will flourish in average soil.

▲ *Salvia xsuperba* 'Mainacht' and *Nepeta racemosa* 'Walker's Low'. Intermingling here creates a very subtle effect, that of two very similar colours ebbing and flowing across space. Similarity in height, habit and flower shape reduces any sense of difference in how we see the plants, so the mind is free to register subtle colour differences.

91

► This is a complex picture created by a profusion of different plant species. However, a fundamental sense of unity is created by the use of grasses and sedges (the lush green in the foreground is the sedge *Carex muskingumensis*) and the repetition of rounded flower-heads, such as that of the maroon *Angelica gigas*, also in the foreground, and of *Sanguisorba officinalis* (left).

93

▲ The seedheads of *Allium cristophii* are highly effective emerging from other plants, here from clumps of *Eryngium bourgatii*. Groups of *Echinacea purpurea* in the background.

Small clumps of flowering perennials surround a large mass of *Calamagrostis xacutiflora* 'Karl Foerster'. The pink (lower right and upper left) is *Eupatorium purpureum* subsp. *maculatum* 'Atropurpureum', the scarlet is *Monarda* 'Squaw' and the cream (right) is *Persicaria polymorpha*. This is the kind of planting which appears to be a solid mass, but in fact is riven by a series of small paths. ▲

where very simple, bold plantings with little complexity, but a strong rhythm, are most appropriate. In these public situations only a few species are needed to create an impact, and it is here that we might argue the case for planting in blocks or drifts. It is worth remembering that this style is interpreted by many as being more 'gardened' and in many cases as more coherent than intermingling – most people find it easier to understand and make visual sense of a block of one plant than an intermingled complex of several species.

In a large landscape, such as a public park, the repetition of blocks of at least 3 m (10 ft) wide are one of the most effective ways of making a visual impact – but the larger the landscape, the larger the blocks need to be. Practical reasons for using blocks of plants include the fact that they are easier for unskilled staff to comprehend: it is simple to teach maintenance staff that each block has to stay as it is. Plants of different levels of competitiveness are separated, which makes it easier to restrain the more vigorous. Additionally they look simple on paper, so people can understand the plans more readily.

• *Approaches to intermingling*

Interspersing blocks of intermingled plant varieties with blocks of monoculture is also a way of ensuring strong visual impact: it gets the message across that the intermingling is deliberate rather than random or accidental. Even more emphatic is when intermingling is juxtaposed with clipped woody plants. This is an extension of the 'creative tension' that results from having long meadow grass adjacent to topiary or geometric hedging, the latter often being seen in baroque gardens in central Europe, or in the Great Dixter garden discussed above.

There are, of course, degrees of intermingling. The most coherent, in terms of its legibility to the general public, and the most self-consciously artistic, is the combination of just two or three varieties chosen for their combined impact, as in the Piet Oudolf borders at Wisley. A greater number of varieties is used in the 'mixed planting' approach. This has a lot of potential for the wilder, more naturalistic end of the spectrum, and offers considerable scope to the amateur gardener or design professional with a

▲ Mingling certain colours, such as the pink of *Echinacea pallida*, *E.* 'Vintage Wine' and the blue of *Perovskia atriplicifolia* can create startling effects.

particular interest in, and knowledge of, plants. In order to give it some structure, however, care needs to be taken to select plants that will complement each other. Selecting plants according to ecological as well as aesthetic criteria is absolutely vital for highly intermingled plantings, as there will be little opportunity to pay much attention to individual plant needs. In particular, they must not compete destructively with each other; for example, a strongly spreading species is clearly not a good companion to one that is slow-growing, and those that collapse after flowering may smother their neighbours. The best way to be reasonably confident that plants have some chance of compatibility is to select species from similar environments.

Species from resource-rich environments such as prairies or wetlands tend to be vigorous and competitive; those from resource-poor ones, such as dry or thin soils, are likely to be slower-growing and less competitive. It follows that the latter may actually require less management to prevent more vigorous species taking over – resource-poor environments, in other words, may more readily support a higher level of diversity and a higher level of complexity, which is often good news in design terms.

• *Minimalism*

Minimalism has been in and out of fashion for a long time, but is difficult to keep up in a consumer society where there is always the temptation to buy more. In gardening real minimalism is rare, as few gardeners really have the discipline to limit themselves to just a few plants or items. In addition it is worth remembering that 'less is more, but only if you know more', in the sense that when few plants are used they have to be right both visually and for the prevailing conditions. Without rejecting the idea of minimalist gardens, we see very few examples that really work, and are sceptical of

▶ Box is a very traditional material for keeping clipped. Used in swirling curves instead of straight lines, it avoids feeling old-fashioned and creates an experience of cool and timeless continuity at the Morton Arboretum, Illinois. The tree is a flowering apple – *Malus floribunda*.

how much the public really want them. However, it is worth remembering the use of minimalism as a design element *within* gardens. It is a good way of changing the pace in a garden – like the sorbet course in an elaborate meal, something to cleanse the palate between other stronger tastes and sensations. Gardens full of complexity are highly stimulating environments – it is all too easy to experience visual and mental overload. Public spaces, in particular, need to offer options between high and low levels of emotional experience.

In looking at highly complex intermingled planting, or indeed even at less complex blended combinations of two or three varieties, it at first seems that these are the complete opposite of minimalism. But it all depends on scale. In a small garden where a planting is on a reduced scale and we inevitably see it from near by, there may be nothing minimalist about it. But on a larger scale, the components will blur together and the whole will become visually far more unified. This is why it is possible to argue that species-rich meadows can be minimalist elements in the landscape, at least at a larger scale. As a thought experiment, contrast them with the appearance of conventional borders at this scale, where there is so much more distracting detail.

▼ Hedges (this is beech, *Fagus sylvatica*) and lawn
make for an atmosphere which is a good contrast
to colourful or complex plantings. This cooling effect
is one of the most useful aspects of minimalism in
the garden.

▲ Blocks of perennials create minimalistic effects,
although if flowers are used the season may be limited.
The deep blue *Salvia* x*superba* 'Mainacht' has a long
flowering season, however. The silver foliage is not a
perennial but the silver pear, *Pyrus salicifolia* 'Pendula'.

Shrubs and trees for formal clipping

Buxus microphylla, B. sempervirens	*Nothofagus antarctica*
Carpinus betula	*Osmanthus delavayi*
Cornus mas	*Podocarpus* (small-leaved species)
Euonymus japonicus 'Microphyllus'	*Prunus lusitanica*
Fagus sylvatica	*Pyrus salicifolia* 'Pendula'
Ilex aquifolium and hybrids; *I. crenata, I. glabra*	*Taxus* species
Ligustrum ovalifolium, L. vulgare	*Tilia* species

Hedges are one way to inject a note of minimalism into gardens. The relative simplicity of the foliage acts as a foil for crowded and informal perennial planting and provides the coherence to balance the borders' complexity. Yew, box and other easily clipped and shaped plants can be used in a contemporary way, and it is surprising to see how little this is done. These species are particularly useful for creating substantial blocks of green which are very simple in outline, but whose continuity, bulk and simplicity offer a total contrast to wispy, ever-changing, highly complex perennial borders.

At ground level, mass planting of grasses and grass-like plants such as species of carex and luzula can also be used to create a similar effect. Luzula, most carex species and some grasses are evergreen, which is particularly useful since the effect of evergreens is to 'ground' a planting in continuity through time. In shadier areas, or colder latitudes, woodland ground-cover plants with dark evergreen foliage (such as varieties of vinca or ivy) can be used to create low textured blocks of green. In climate zones with warm, humid summers, fine-leaved species of liriope and its close relative ophiopogon are frequently used. Plants with larger or more distinct leaves, such as bergenias or hostas, are less suitable because their leaves create a more detailed texture and therefore increase complexity.

Minimalism often has a use in providing a sense of continuity, which can be particularly valuable when there are either major seasonal changes in plantings or many very disparate elements. This is worth bearing in mind for plant collectors, whose love of assembling plants for their own sakes militates powerfully against any sense of artistic unity. An example of how this can work in practice can be seen at Scampston Hall, an Oudolf project in the walled garden of a country house in Yorkshire, England. Here a 350 m (1000 ft) lime walk provides the minimalist element, unifying a series of plant collections along the way into a simple design that effectively integrates a wide variety of disparate material.

97

Plants with a long season of interest

*** very good structure from spring to late winter

** good all-round character for much of the season

* distinctive but for a shorter period

L long flowering season of 4–6 weeks

R repeat-flowering, especially if cut back

W distinctive and long-lasting seedheads and/or winter skeleton

C good autumn colour depending on season and region

Perennials

Acaena species	***		W	
Achillea species	***	R	W	
Aconitum species	*			
Actaea species	***		W	
Agastache species	***	L	W	
Amsonia species	***		W	C
Anaphalis species	***	L	W	
Anemone cylindrica, A. xhybrida	***	L	W	
Artemisia lactiflora	**		W	
Aruncus species	**		W	C
Asclepias species	**		W	
Asphodeline species	**		W	
Aster xfrikartii 'Mönch', *A.* 'Twilight'	**	L		
Aster umbellatus	**		W	
Astilbe species	***		W	
Astrantia species	*	L		
Baptisia species	*		W	
Calamintha species	***	L	W	
Campanula latifolia	**		W	
Cephalaria species	**		W	
Chelone species	***		W	
Cirsium rivulare 'Atropurpureum'	**	L R		
Clematis integrifolia, C. recta	**		W	
Coreopsis species	**	L	W	C
C. tripteris	**	L	W	C
Cynara species	***		W	
Darmera peltata	**			C
Dictamnus albus	**		W	
Digitalis ferruginea, D. parviflora	***		W	
D. lanata	***		W	
Echinacea species	***	L	W	
Echinops species	**		W	
Eryngium species	***		W	
Eupatorium (tall types)	***		W	C
Euphorbia species	*			C
Ferula species	**		W	
Filipendula species	**		W	

		L	R	W	C
Geranium wallichianum 'Buxton's Variety',					
G. nodosum	*	L			
G. endressii, G. xoxonianum	*	L	R		
G. ROZANNE 'Gerwat'	**	L			
G. sanguineum	*	L			C
G. soboliferum, G. wlassovianum	*				C
Gillenia trifoliata	***			W	C
Glaucium species	**	L		W	
Gypsophila species	**			W	
Helenium species	***	L		W	
Heuchera villosa	**			W	C
Hosta species	**				C
Inula hookeri	**			W	
Iris ensata, I. sibirica	**			W	
Knautia macedonica	***	L			
Kniphofia (some)	*	L			
Lavatera cachemiriana	**	L		W	
Liatris species	***			W	
Ligularia species	*			W	
Limonium platyphyllum	**			W	
Lobelia xspeciosa 'Vedrariensis'	**	L			
Lunaria rediviva	**	L		W	
Lychnis chalcedonica	*				C
Lysimachia clethroides	*				C
Lysimachia ephemerum	**			W	C
Lythrum species	**	L		W	C
Malva moschata	*			W	
Monarda species	***			W	
Nepeta 'Six Hills Giant' & similar	**		R		
Origanum species	***	L		W	
Paeonia species	**			W	C
Perovskia species	***	L		W	
Persicaria amplexicaulis, P. polymorpha	**	L			
Phlomis species	***			W	
Rodgersia species	***			W	
Rudbeckia species	***			W	
Salvia nemorosa, S. xsuperba	**		R		
Sanguisorba canadensis	**	L			C

		L		W	C
Scutellaria species	**			W	
Sedum species	***			W	
Selinum species	**			W	
Seseli species	**			W	
Silphium species	***			W	C
Stachys species	***			W	
Thalictrum lucidum, T. pubescens	***			W	C
Thermopsis species	**			W	
Tricyrtis species	**	L			C
Trifolium rubens	**			W	
Veratrum species	***			W	C
Verbascum species	***			W	
Verbena species	**			W	
Veronica longifolia, V. spicata	**			W	
Veronicastrum species	***			W	C

Grasses

		L		W	C
Calamagrostis xacutiflora	**			W	
Calamagrostis brachytricha	***			W	
Chasmanthium latifolium	**			W	
Deschampsia cespitosa	***	L		W	
Eragrostis spectabilis	***			W	C
Hakonechloa macra	***			W	C
Miscanthus species	***			W	C
Molinia species	***			W	C
Panicum species	***			W	C
Pennisetum species	**			W	C
Schizachyrium scoparium	**			W	C
Sorghastrum nutans	**			W	C
Stipa species	***			W	

Ferns

					C
Onoclea sensibilis	**				C
Osmunda species	***				C

The mechanics of planting design

◄ Fertile soils and plentiful moisture support lush, late-flowering perennials, many of which should be valued for their structure as much as their colour. Here, from the foreground backwards, *Veronicastrum virginicum* 'Roseum', the globes of *Echinops sphaerocephalus*, yellow *Thalictrum lucidum* (right), and pink *Eupatorium purpureum* subsp. *maculatum* 'Atropurpureum'.

Is it possible to learn design skills? Or are they intuitive? Perhaps the question is only partly relevant, as even gifted people will always have to learn how to use their material. Our intention here is not to provide a step-by-step guide to designing a planting, but instead to suggest a series of processes which we consider particularly relevant to the key issues of plant selection and combination. We stress those elements such as the use of structure which we feel are often overlooked. We suggest how to select plants and give some basic indications as to how they can be combined; what happens then is up to you – individual intuition and creativity will take over.

We are great believers in lists. Compiling lists of ecologically and aesthetically compatible plants is a huge step towards a successful design, more crucial indeed than their exact placement. This is demonstrated by the visual success of some very well established ecological plantings where natural processes have so shuffled the original plant selection that the outcome is only partly a result of human design.

Ecological and aesthetic criteria

So many plants are now available from nurseries, and the potential for using them in creative design is enormous and getting greater. We all have favourite plants, and our ability to use these is a large part of the success we have with our gardens. But there is a danger of getting stuck in a rut and always using the same plants. For this reason we strongly advise casting the net wide in selecting plants. A planting scheme will be much the stronger if all possibilities are considered rather than just a few. Start off with lists of all possible species derived from reference books and nursery catalogues, and then narrow them down. This approach tends to confront you with plants that perhaps you may not have thought of, and therefore encourages creativity.

► Winter in the short-grass prairie area at Hermanns-hof, with frost emphasizing plant structure. A yucca species, native to the high altitude desert areas of the western USA, with a variety of grasses and perennials.

101

For any given proposed planting, you need two basic lists – one based on ecological criteria and the other on aesthetic ones. Ecology must come first – artistic factors can be looked at only once we have a list of what will grow. To succeed long-term, plants have to thrive, which means that their ecological requirements (for particular levels of light, moisture, nutrients and so on) must be met by the site. Gardeners in the past were much more prepared to defy ecology and to provide extensive irrigation, feed annually, take plants under cover in the winter and generally interfere with nature. Many of these practices are now regarded as increasingly unsustainable as we learn to husband the planet's resources more carefully.

Ecological criteria can be wide or narrow, depending on the locality. There are geographic regions where climate allows a large number of plants to be grown, and on the other hand, harsh climates may impose considerable limitations. Even in the former, there are individual gardens where poor soil conditions impose major constraints. To summarize very crudely:

mild climate	harsh climate
good growing conditions	demanding growing conditions
wide plant range	narrow plant range
long growing season	short growing season
mild winters	cold winters
cool summers	hot summers
drought or waterlogging rare	drought or waterlogging common
extreme weather events rare	likelihood of extreme weather
soil fertility good	soil fertility low

▼ It's colourful but how good is it on a structural level? Taking a black and white photograph is a simple way to assess how structure is working, as it cuts out the colour from our consideration of what we see. It is surprising just how muddy many otherwise good-looking borders can seem. Here deep mauve-pink *Stachys officinalis* 'Hummelo', *Nepeta racemosa* 'Walker's Low' and the grass *Calamagrostis brachytricha* provide structural as well as colour interest.

Where environmental conditions are relaxed and it is possible to grow a wide range of plants, there is little need for strict ecological criteria, and it is possible to be eclectic and choose species from a wide range of different habitats, with plants from the steppe

▲ These *Achillea* hybrids, including 'Walther Funcke' (middle of picture) and 'Summerwine' (foreground) are wonderfully colourful plants, but short-lived and unlikely to survive the winter on soils which do not drain sharply. They seem to thrive better in more continental climates, too. Between the achilleas is a *Sedum spectabile* cultivar which, despite originating in dry habitats, is much more long-lived and resilient.

alongside plants from moist meadows. Where conditions are harsher, then only those plants which have a good ecological fit to the prevailing conditions will survive, and the first task will be to make a list on this basis. Plant reference books will be the first port of call – some harsh-climate zones have a good gardening literature, which can be immensely useful. In such areas, the advice of nurseries and of other gardeners can also be very valuable. In those lucky areas where a very wide range of plants can be grown, only the most fundamental of environmental conditions need be paid attention to – sunny or shady and moist or dry.

Predicting climate with certainty is, of course, impossible, and there is always some risk involved. To a lesser extent this also applies to a plant's reaction to soil type and local microclimate. Gardeners like to take risks, and indeed this has almost become fashionable as growers of the exotic push the boundaries of what can be grown. The level of risk that can be taken depends more or less directly on the relative softness or severity of the local climate. Gardeners in severe climate areas can afford to take fewer risks than those in places where dry summers or cold winters are rare. However, no sensible gardener uses plants for key roles in their work if there is any chance that they will not survive; a good design relies for its main effect on species which are totally dependable.

There are key differences in appearance between the range of plants which can be grown in good conditions and those from places where climate and soil make for harsher conditions. Species from generous environments tend to be green and lush, with large, soft leaves and generous, expansive growth, whereas those from harsher conditions tend to have a tighter habit of growth and smaller, tougher leaves that are very often not green; those from dry environments in particular have a grey or silver cast to their foliage. This clearly has an impact on the aesthetics of possible plant combinations; gardeners with good growing conditions can combine both lush- and tough-looking plants; those in more demanding sites will be more limited. Incidentally, stress-tolerant plants are far more likely to be evergreen.

Lists based on aesthetic criteria are potentially far more complex – for a start they will be subjective rather than objective. If you want a strong overall theme, one based on colour for example, or one that makes effective use of large foliage, or grasses or locally native plants, then it makes sense to draw up lists based on these criteria early on. Where it is considered desirable to include native plants or species attractive to wildlife, it is sensible to make up a separate list of possibilities, bearing in mind that some may be inferior visually to non-native species. Having several lists allows you to see where the overlaps are, those plants which occur in more than one list clearly being particularly useful.

Then it is a question of translating the lists into a physical object. A good planting involves achieving a harmonious balance between a variety of structural elements. In any wild habitat there will be plants with different growth forms; a forest, for example, may be dominated by trees, but may also include shrubs, climbers and ground-level herbaceous plants. A meadow is more uniform, but may include grasses with both spreading and tussock- or clump-forming habits, as well as upright and clump-forming herbaceous plants and some climbing or sprawling ones. Achieving a successful planting, in both visual and functional terms, depends upon balancing these elements. Structural plants make up the majority of the biomass of a planting, and therefore dictate how it will look for the bulk of the year. In contrast colour, whether of flower or leaf, is superficial, and although it may make an immediate impact, it is the underlying structure that will really make a planting a success or not.

Woody plants for structure

Woody plants take up so much more space than herbaceous species, and selecting them is in many ways a more serious business – the consequences of a bad decision are far greater. Much tree and shrub planting is involved with the macro scale of the garden – dividing up space, creating screens etc. Here we are concerned with their role at a smaller scale, where they will be in close proximity to many other plants. Perhaps the best way to approach considerations of woody plant selection is to look at the relative importance of their role on three different types of situation.

WOODY-PLANT PRIORITY | Where a large-scale design requires the planting of trees or shrubs, then perennials and other elements have to fit in around them, and in time, as the woody plants mature, the perennials may be lost. An example might be an avenue where underplanting is wanted, or a narrow border along a hedge. In these situations, the selection of the trees or shrubs takes priority and other plant species are chosen which will be compatible with them. A key issue is that of development over time, as the growing trees or shrubs will cast ever-increasing shade and gradually compete more effectively for moisture and nutrients with surrounding plants.

WOODY PLANTS IN BALANCE | Characteristic of many English-style gardens from the 1960s onwards are mixed borders that aim to combine small trees, shrubs and perennials (and, of course, bulbs and often annuals too). This has undoubtedly been an

▼ Good reasons for including *Mahonia xmedia* 'Charity' in a planting are its interesting foliage, long season and winter flowers. In smaller gardens, the few shrubs used need to earn their keep.

Hydrangea aspera is another example of a shrub that fits in well with perennials. It does not spread strongly and has impressively large leaves which contrast well with the smaller foliage of most perennials. ▼

Digitalis ferruginea ▼ is one of the finest biennials for winter interest, with tall and narrow seedheads which create a ghostly effect in certain weather conditions.

◄ The tight whorls of the flowerheads of monardas are an effective contrast to the wispy heads of the grass *Molinia*. Such gentle contrasts are the lifeblood of good herbaceous planting design.

105

immensely influential garden style internationally, and it has particular benefits for biodiversity, offering a wide range of ecological niches for wildlife. We could argue, however, that it can lack a certain discipline, particularly when dominated by the amorphous shapes of untrained shrubs. Nevertheless, in certain situations – particularly in large gardens or public spaces – this is a style of great value.

WOODY PLANTS FOR SPECIFIC PURPOSES | In a planting dominated by perennials with good form, the role of woody plants is a relatively subsidiary one, and they should be chosen for the particular contribution they make to the overall design. An example might be the upright white stems of *Rubus thibetanus* for winter interest, or a hamamelis for flower colour and fragrance in early spring. Qualities that woody plants can contribute include seasonal continuity, as unlike herbaceous plants they are always visually present; the structural factor of size and bulk, and flowers or interesting foliage features during winter and early spring.

Herbaceous plants and structure

We see good plant structure as central to planting design, and are keen to emphasize this in the way we categorize plants, and in particular to draw the attention of designers and the garden public to the structural opportunities offered by herbaceous plants. Our definition of a structural plant is somewhat wider than that of many other writers on gardens – we may see structure where others see nothing beyond flower colour. Good structure plants are what really makes a combination of herbaceous perennials successful. Long-lasting plants with strong shapes provide a framework of continuity, often until well into the winter. We are particularly keen to draw the attention of gardeners and designers to those plants that have good structure after flowering – of which the list is extensive (see pages 98 and 99).

Different designers make different distinctions in the way they use plants for structure, depending upon how they work. Here we discuss a variety of categories in order to show how awareness of structure can be used as a basis for different ways of combining plants. Essentially we recognize a hierarchy of structure in plantings, and discuss the respective roles of solitary plants; dominant structure plants; bulk structure plants; filler plants and strewing plants.

SOLITARY PLANTS are those which just have to be on their own, because they are visually ineffective if surrounded by too many neighbours of their own height. They are rather like prima donnas – magnificent but highly-strung, and needing space around them to be fully appreciated. They generally have an upright habit and a very distinctive structure over a long season. Examples include large grasses, *Dictamnus albus, Eupatorium purpureum* subsp. *maculatum* and *Inula magnifica*. In larger settings, the repetition of a solitary plant can make a particularly powerful statement; in smaller ones, they provide good 'bones'.

DOMINANT STRUCTURE PLANTS are those with good and distinctive structure over a long season. Their structure may be an aspect of their overall form, of bold or distinct

▲ Good structure and backlighting combine to create a highly attractive picture of *Verbascum lychnitis* and, in the background, *Peucedanum verticillare*. On the left is the grass *Stipa gigantea*.

Tulipa hageri 'Splendens' is one of many species tulips which make good 'strewing plants' to scatter around between larger plants for a quick spring show. ▲

foliage, or of their flower- or seedheads. Among them, grasses are increasingly recognized by designers and the public as key plants. What grasses offer in terms of structure is actually very variable. In most cases it is firmness and stature, although this is almost inevitably linked to softness and elegance.

Umbellifers belong here, their value lying in their generally long-lived form rather than flower colour. Plants with flowers in spikes, such as verbascums and digitalis, can be among the most eye-catching, but in nearly all cases they are effective only if grouped or planted closely enough to be seen as relating to each other – one on its own simply looks lonely.

BULK STRUCTURAL PLANTS | The mass of a visually successful border is made up of plants with definite structural qualities, but which are not so emphatic that they demand our immediate attention. For this reason, perhaps, their value has often been disregarded, or they have conventionally been rated for other aspects, usually flower colour. Yet these plants are the mainstay of those plantings which genuinely provide a long season of interest. Their value is that they have enough structural qualities to sustain interest through most of the growing season, but not so much that they are in danger of competing with each other (as sometimes happens in the gardens of those who are addicted to collecting exotic-looking plants).

Most later-flowering herbaceous plants can be included in this category, as they have at the very least a quiet tidy beauty in the months before they flower and very often a distinct structural value afterwards. Asters are a good example, forming a neat mound of foliage which at flowering time develops into a characteristic shape for each species. After flowering most asters look at least passable for a while, and some, such as *A. umbellatus*, are quite distinctive. Some less structural lower-growing grasses belong here, among them *Eragrostis spectabilis* and *Sesleria autumnalis*. Quite apart from the qualities of their flower-heads, plants with linear foliage like iris, crocosmia, kniphofia and grasses are particularly useful for changing the pace of a planting, offering a break from the mass of small nondescript foliage that can sometimes dominate in a border.

107

▼ Some plants, like this *Inula magnifica* 'Sonnenstrahl', are best seen when looked up at – they become more imposing, and the extraordinarily narrow ray-florets are best appreciated from this angle.

FILLER PLANTS | Many herbaceous plants, generally earlier-flowering ones, fall into this category. Whatever virtues they may possess, they have the disadvantage of either being amorphous or becoming so after flowering, and having no winter interest whatsoever. Of course, the notion of structure plants and filler plants is to some extent a relative one. It is possible for the same plant to have quite a different role in different situations: for example, a short grass with good structure is only a front-of-border or filler plant in a planting dominated by tall plants, but in a much lower planting it could be a dominant structure plant. Of those plants which do not maintain good structure through the season, many have at least some structural role early on; who, for example, is not impressed by the neat hemispheres of geraniums in spring?

Hardy geraniums are undoubtedly plants of enormous garden and landscape value in this category, especially for mild, maritime-influenced climates. The range of high-quality species and hybrids now available is enormous, and they are extremely popular. However, they can flop unattractively after flowering, often crushing later-developing perennials beneath them. Here are some suggestions for making effective use of filler plants and other relatively structureless early-flowering perennials:

- On a domestic scale, plants can be supported with pea-sticks, or cut down after flowering and left to regrow, which they will do given sufficient midsummer moisture – although a temporary and unattractive gap is inevitable. Quite a few varieties will repeat-flower in late summer or early autumn.
- In borders they may be included as a minority element to provide interest from late spring to early summer, but should have as neighbours enough good-quality later-flowering species to draw attention from their deficiencies for the rest of the season.
- In larger plantings, or in situations such as shade where the number of later-flowering perennials may be restricted, they can be grown as a kind of glorified ground cover, a planting with little structural interest but plenty of early summer colour. The best way of managing them is to cut them all back in midsummer after their main flowering season; within a month they will have regrown enough to look respectable, and some species will repeat-flower.
- Early-flowering filler plants can be grouped in such a way that they are concealed from view by others which develop later. In shady situations this may be achieved with the limited number of very attractive, taller-growing, late-flowering plants such as aconitums, actaeas and Japanese anemones.
- In wild-garden or public-park situations, the messy mid-season demise of plants in this category does not really matter, provided that some other species are included for additional interest.

STREWING PLANTS are those small plants with no real bulk that may be scattered around – bulbs and other geophytes for spring interest, or small self-sowing annuals for summer. Their interest may be low-level, but they do much to bring life to gardens in spring. Generally, they look best if their distribution is more or less random, or in loose clumps as they would grow in nature. In practice, though, they will need to be positioned between perennial clumps.

▲ The shape of the flower-heads of the midsummer-flowering *Sanguisorba tenuifolia* 'Alba' have structure and colour, at least when lit from behind or from the side and seen against a dark background.

► Eryngiums (this is *Eryngium yuccifolium*) are nearly always dominant structural plants, as their dramatic shapes always seize the attention of the onlooker.

THE MECHANICS OF PLANTING DESIGN

▼ *Eragrostis spectabilis* is another grass which looks magical in autumn, its fine seedheads making a good counterpoint to more defined structures.

▲ Grasses – this is *Sporobolus heterolepis* – are invaluable for structure and continuity. It is the soft appearance of this one which makes it so attractive, as well as, unusually for a grass, a lot of sweet scent in the flowering period.

▼ *Geranium xcantabrigiense* is an example of a plant whose wide environmental tolerance and vigorous growth means it is often over-used as a ground cover. More imaginative planting in combination with some other species would bring out its good points.

In addition, smaller-growing annuals and biennials can be used as strewing plants, particularly in the first year for temporary gap filling. Vigorously sideways-spreading annuals should be avoided, however, as they can swamp slower-growing perennials and take over visually. Less vigorous species with an upright habit, such as nigella or linums, are more appropriate.

• *Matrix plantings*
These are where a single species dominates a planting, forming a matrix into which other species are blended. This is usually seen in situations where extensive ground cover is needed, but where something more interesting than a solid green monoculture is desired. Either a single species, or a small number of similar species – always with definite structural interest – is used to cover most of the ground, with others added for

► Intermingled grasses and perennials can create some very effective scenes. Here the silvery-looking grass is *Calamagrostis brachytricha* with the seedheads of *Veronicastrum virginicum* 'Temptation' and the occasional *Perovskia atriplicifolia* in late summer.

▲ *Actaea simplex* 'James Compton' and *Molinia caerulea* subsp. *arundinacea* 'Cordoba' make a fine combination in late summer or early autumn.

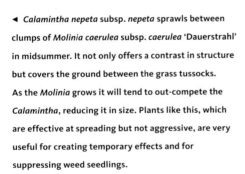

◄ *Calamintha nepeta* subsp. *nepeta* sprawls between clumps of *Molinia caerulea* subsp. *caerulea* 'Dauerstrahl' in midsummer. It not only offers a contrast in structure but covers the ground between the grass tussocks. As the *Molinia* grows it will tend to out-compete the *Calamintha*, reducing it in size. Plants like this, which are effective at spreading but not aggressive, are very useful for creating temporary effects and for suppressing weed seedlings.

contrast and extra interest. In shady spots, species of carex or luzula are often very successful, combined with pulmonarias, smaller geraniums such as *G. nodosum* and bulbs. In more open situations, this style of planting is rarely seen, although it has considerable potential, particularly for stylized meadow effects based on plants such as *Deschampsia cespitosa* and *Sporobolus heterolepis*.

Designing combinations

Designers need to be clear about which approach to combining plants they are using. We would argue that *all* the plants in a design should look good together, so that even if they fell together at random, there would still be interest and harmony. But striking juxtapositions are also important, particularly in key places where onlookers will be able to appreciate them.

People use various criteria to combine plants. The most common is based on colour: innumerable books have been written on the subject, and many theories advanced, but in the end views on colour are inevitably subjective. We would point out that the importance of colour combining is to some extent dependent upon the type of plants used. Highly bred hybrids have a high proportion of flower to foliage and therefore a relatively large expanse of colour in a given unit area – so with these plants getting colours right is important. However, with the more natural range of plants we prefer to use, there is relatively more foliage, so colours are more widely separated and more diluted in the field of vision. Matching them is therefore markedly less important.

Combining on the basis of plant shape is also an approach which many designers use, although somewhat subconsciously, and this topic has not been articulated and discussed anything like as much as colour-based schemes. In our Designing with Plants we proposed Piet's system of combining on the basis of plant, leaf and flower shapes. To summarize, any system of combining with shapes is about creating a balance between contrast (which generates visual stimulation) and harmony (which creates a feeling of rest). Here are few pointers:

113

- A variety of shapes creates interest.
- Upright shapes (spire-shaped flower-heads, narrow upright trees) act as 'exclamation marks' and attract attention; their repetition creates a particularly strong effect.
- Distinctive shapes, such as the spiky rosettes of yuccas or sculptural plants like eryngiums, are perceived as dramatic.
- Rounded shapes (such as low hummocky shrubs) are perceived as restful, particularly if repeated.
- Herbaceous plants in particular have a wide variety of textures, ranging from the very diffuse, like the larger molinia grasses, to the very defined, such as the tight flower-heads of monardas and phlomis. These can be used to create layered effects by positioning tightly defined shapes in front of or behind diffuse, effectively 'transparent', plants.

• Combining structural plant categories

A crucially important topic is that of combining the plant categories we have just been discussing. The overall appearance of a planting, and indeed details of its management, are very dependent on the proportions used of plants from these categories. Traditional perennial-based planting schemes such as herbaceous borders, with their emphasis on flower colour, much of it contributed by hybrids, did not put much stress on structure. As a consequence they would often look uninspired until the main (rather late) flowering season, and frequently a mess afterwards.

A general rule of Piet's is that the proportion of structural plants to filler plants should be around 70:30 in terms of ground area covered. This high proportion of structural plants can be applied to a wide variety of habitats. For shade and for moist sites there are a great many plants with bold or distinctive foliage rather than a clear overall shape, and using them at this 70:30 percentage creates a strong and long-lasting structure. Dry habitats feature many species with strong structure, too, but

The seedheads of *Phlomis tuberosa* with the flowers of *Lobelia xspeciosa* 'Vedrariensis', *Lavatera cachemiriana* and *Verbena hastata* – the first very strongly structural, over a long period, the others having some structural interest over a much shorter span. ▼

▼ *Echinacea pallida* with, behind it, *Veronicastrum virginicum* 'Fascination' and, to the left, the grass *Calamagrostis xacutiflora* 'Karl Foerster'. All are strongly structural plants, with a season of interest which lasts well after their flowering.

▲ More exciting structural plants: the globes of *Echinops sphaerocephalus* with white *Agastache foeniculum* 'Alba' and the grass molinia. But be warned: the *Echinops* seedheads do not last long, disintegrating in early winter.

derived more from plant form than foliage shape; think of the effective contrasts between hummocky sub-shrubs like lavenders and spiky rosette-formers such as yuccas. The poorest selection of strong structure plants is probably found among the flora of the woodland edge and the averagely moist open habitats of cool temperate regions. To put it another way, this is perhaps where there is the greatest temptation to use plants with high 'flower power' but poor structure. The dominant semi-natural plant community of many such places is grass-dominated meadow or prairie. Wild grasses do have strong structure; European meadow ones at least until midsummer, North American prairie ones from midsummer onwards, which points the designer towards using plenty of them.

The German practitioners who developed the Silbersommer mixture and other mixed-planting combinations define plants according to categories: Solitary plants 10 per cent; Group perennials 40-50 per cent; Ground-cover plants 40-50 per cent.

The group perennials are those such as species of aster, achillea, euphorbia, filipendula and nepeta which form distinct clumps. Most of these have good structure, due more to their flower-head shapes than their overall form, and these correspond to our category of 'bulk structure plants' above. Others, however, are what we would dub 'fillers'. They tend to dominate the planting visually, forming the bulk of the vegetation and defining its average height. In addition, strewing plants can be added in varying proportions, depending on plant size and length of season of interest; species like crocuses which are very ephemeral can be planted relatively densely.

115

▲ A gravel garden at Bury Court, Hampshire, uses
Mediterranean-climate and other dry-zone plants,
exploiting their neat compact shapes, repeating them
and contrasting them with other looser or sharper
forms.

Laying out plants

The positioning of plants is the most intuitively driven part of the planting process, for
which few rules can be given. Designers almost inevitably start with the most strongly
structural plants and work down to the filler plants, ground cover and strewing plants.

It is vital to know how far apart plants should be placed. Usually it is possible to
discover a plant's spread from reference books or nursery catalogues, although this can
vary wildly between different sites and climate zones. As a general rule, you should
imagine a figure for the spread of a herbaceous plant as the diameter of a circle with
the plant in the centre. For medium-sized and larger shrubs, where growth to a mature
size will be much slower, it can be safely assumed that a metre- or yard-wide circle free
of other plants will be enough for the shrub to establish itself.

Plant numbers are calculated differently depending upon whether the species used
is going to be grouped or intermingled. Individuals of a single species in a group can be
planted relatively closely together, whereas when they are intermingled, inter-species
competition is more intense, and if they are too closely spaced, the gradual elimination
of some species may be expected. The spaces between groups also need to be wider
than those between the individuals in the groups for the same reason. Species which
spread or form bushy clumps need to be given more space around them at planting
than less vigorous or definitely upright species.

It is a common mistake, not just of beginners, to include too many plant varieties
and ending up with a bitty, unfocused planting. A rule recommended by many
designers is to try to reduce the number of varieties once the first draft of a plan is
complete. (Needless to say this must be done at the planning stage, on paper.)
Remember that larger sites do not always require more plant varieties – indeed they
may well look best with fewer.

▶ Repetition of *Astrantia major* 'Claret' and the
bronze-purple leaves of *Actaea simplex* Atropurpurea
Group across a limited area in early summer makes for
an interesting effect. Young leaf-clumps of *Aster novae-
angliae* 'Violetta' are in the foreground.

► Bulk structure can be provided by clumps of grasses – this is *Calamagrostis brachytricha* – and *Salvia* x*superba* 'Dear Anja' flowering in early summer. Later on, the grass will strengthen its structural presence as it flowers, and the salvia will lose much of its interest, although it may flower again if cut back.

▲ Autumn at Wisley, with masses of *Echinacea purpurea* 'Rubinglow' and, in the background, *Hibiscus moscheutos*. Many perennials look best in autumn or winter in large blocks, which emphasize the impact of their seedheads.

Creating linkages and rhythms

A garden, park or planting becomes a unified whole when it has features which bring together disparate parts. There is no contradiction here between developing a sense of *unity* and creating areas with their own distinct character, as only a few key long-season elements need to be used. The large scale and more or less regular repetition of key structural plants can be used to develop a sense of *rhythm*; strictly regular repetition of something generates a sense of formality and order, while doing so less regularly gives structure to more informal plantings. The density of a rhythmical element can even be used to speed up or slow down the pace of interest, as in music.

Elsewhere we look at how major formal elements such as hedges can be used to create unity in a garden (see page 59). Here we are more concerned with a smaller scale. As a general rule, the stronger the structure of a plant, the more impact it will have, so the fewer will be needed to create a sense of unity. Here we look at how plants from various structural categories can be used:

Solitary plants	major impact – few needed.
Dominant structure plants	ideal for many situations
Filler plants	often contribute only colour, so often a short season, although coloured foliage can be successful for a longer effect
Strewing plants	very effective if used extensively, but only for a short season
Grasses	excellent for structure or visual texure or both, often for most of the season
Evergreens	very useful also for continuity, so effectively dual-purpose; can be dull if used too extensively

From this we can see that the longer the season a plant has, the more useful it will be, creating unity in time as well as in space, but this is not to ignore the value of more ephemeral plants. Bulbs in spring can do much to bring a garden together at a time when the scene is very bare, and self-sowing annuals and biennials can generate a feeling of wildness and spontaneity.

117

119

◄◄ Repetition of clumps of the grass *Deschampsia cespitosa* 'Goldtau' across a wide area creates a very powerful impression of rhythm, encouraging the viewer to look onwards and to see the area surveyed as a whole.

► An example of one of the bands or stripes in the Oudolf borders at Wisley: an intermingling of *Gaura lindheimeri*, *Perovksia atriplicifolia* and the purple spikes of *Lobelia* x*speciosa* 'Tania'. This is an extremely colourful but perhaps not very strongly structural combination.

Simple *repetition* works at a lower level than rhythm. It is about creating connections between one part of a planting and another, but not about integrating and unifying spaces. Repeating an element three or four times provides a quiet sub-rhythm and can unify small spaces; moderately structural plants and coloured foliage are particularly useful. An *echo* is the repetition of one element at some distance to where there is a larger concentration of something. One specimen of a grass such as a calamagrostis species in a border might be a reminder and evocation of a much larger group elsewhere in the garden.

An important question in planning a garden or planting is whether to plan unifying elements such as rhythm, repetition or echoes earlier or later in the design process. For strongly structural elements the answer is clear – right at the beginning, but for less emphatic elements, whose main contribution is colour, there is more flexibility, and annuals and bulbs can be added almost as an afterthought.

Linkages are about mediating between very different-looking plants. Species with an intermediate character between the lower and taller plants used are called for. Soft textures and muted colours are often very effective at linking plants with a very different character, such as feathery grasses creating a connection between the strong

Completely hardy bold foliage plants

Acanthus species	*Inula magnifica*
Anemone x*hybrida*	*Ligularia* species
Angelica archangelica (biennial)	*Macleaya* species
Aralia cachemirica, *A. californica*, *A. cordata*, *A. racemosa*	*Osmunda regalis*
Astilboides tabularis	*Petasites japonicus* (invasive)
Brunnera macrophylla	*Rheum* species
Crambe species	*Rodgersia* species
Darmera peltata	*Silphium* species
Filipendula kamtschatica	*Telekia speciosa*
Heuchera species	*Trachystemon orientalis* (invasive)
Hosta species & varieties	*Veratrum* species

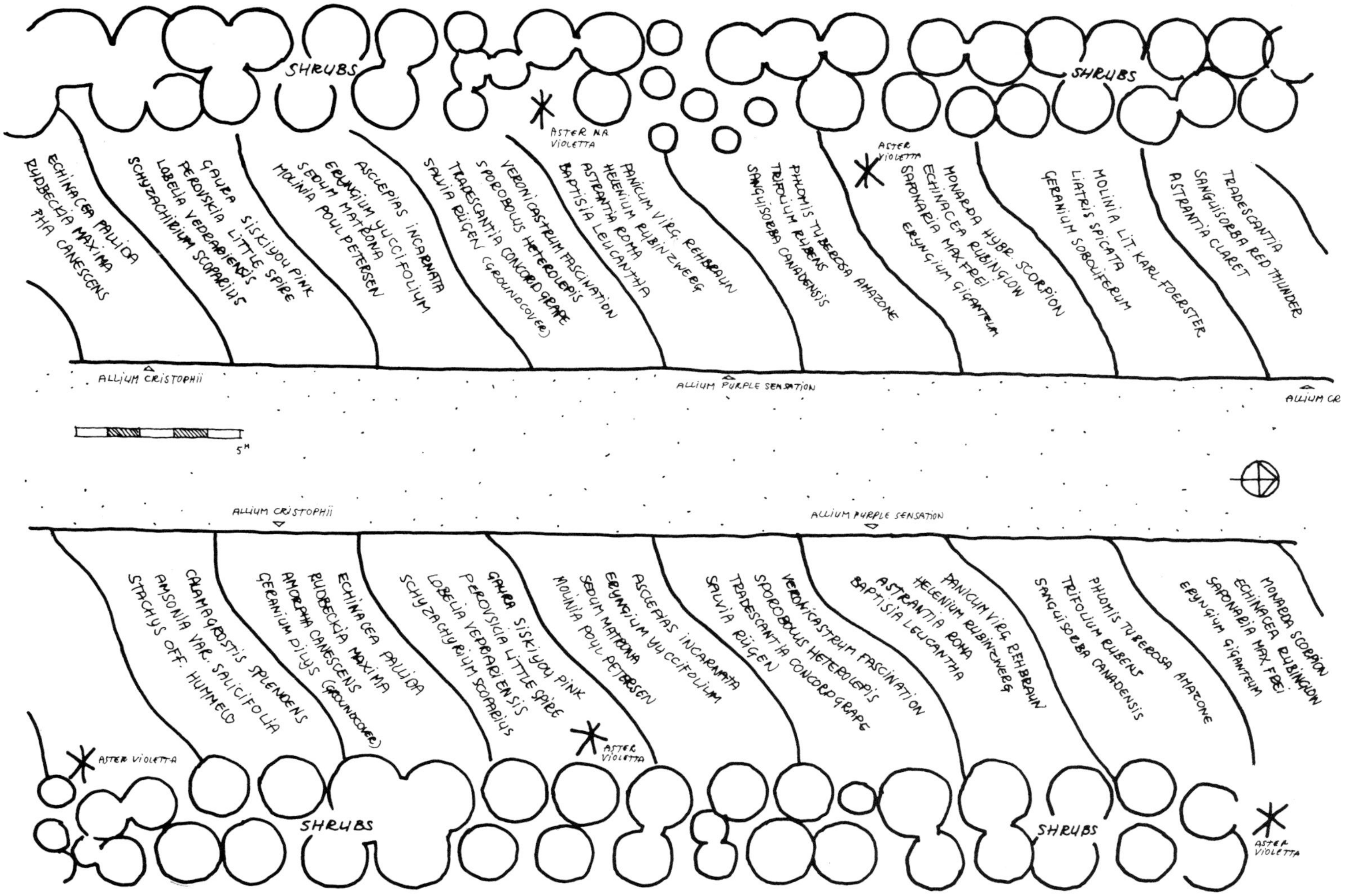
SHRUBS
ASTER NA VIOLETTA
ASTER VIOLETTA
ECHINACEA PALLIDA
RUDBECKIA MAXIMA
PHA CANESCENS
GAURA SISKIYOU PINK
PEROVSKIA LITTLE SPIRE
LOBELIA VEDRARIENSIS
SCHYZACHIRIUM SCOPARIUS
ASCLEPIAS INCARNATA
ERYNGIUM YUCCIFOLIUM
SEDUM MATRONA
MOLINIA POUL PETERSEN
VERONICASTRUM FASCINATION
SPOROBOLUS HETEROLEPIS
TRADESCANTIA CONCORD GRAPE
SALVIA RÜGEN (GROUNDCOVER)
PANICUM VIRG. REHBRAUN
HELENIUM RUBINZWERG
ASTRANTIA ROMA
BAPTISIA LEUCANTHA
PHLOMIS TUBEROSA AMAZONE
TRIFOLIUM RUBENS
SANGUISORBA CANADENSIS
MONARDA HYBR. SCORPION
ECHINACEA RUBINGLOW
SAPONARIA MAX FREI
ERYNGIUM GIGANTEUM
MOLINIA LIT. KARL FOERSTER
LIATRIS SPICATA
GERANIUM SOBOLIFERUM
TRADESCANTIA
SANGUISORBA RED THUNDER
ASTRANTIA CLARET
ALLIUM CRISTOPHII
ALLIUM PURPLE SENSATION
ALLIUM CR
5M
CALAMAGROSTIS SPLENDENS
AMSONIA VAR. SALICIFOLIA
STACHYS OFF. HUMMELO
ECHINACEA PALLIDA
RUDBECKIA MAXIMA
AMORPHA CANESCENS
GERANIUM DILYS (GROUNDCOVER)
GAURA SISKIYOU PINK
PEROVSKIA LITTLE SPIRE
LOBELIA VEDRARIENSIS
SCHYZACHYRIUM SCOPARIUS
ASCLEPIAS INCARNATA
ERYNGIUM YUCCIFOLIUM
SEDUM MATRONA
MOLINIA POUL PETERSEN
VERONICASTRUM FASCINATION
SPOROBOLUS HETEROLEPIS
TRADESCANTIA CONCORD GRAPE
SALVIA RÜGEN
PANICUM VIRG. REHBRAUN
HELENIUM RUBINZWERG
ASTRANTIA ROMA
BAPTISIA LEUCANTHA
PHLOMIS TUBEROSA AMAZONE
TRIFOLIUM RUBENS
SANGUISORBA CANADENSIS
MONARDA SCORPION
ECHINACEA RUBINGLOW
SAPONARIA MAX FREI
ERYNGIUM GIGANTEUM

▲ Every plant with a particularly long season is repeated. Plants have to be distributed across the whole and they have to combine well within the stripe, especially with regard to foliage and height. Each stripe is different, and so no exact combination is repeated. There has to be a balance in each season across the whole area: different colours must be well distributed and nothing should dominate at any particular time. As a general rule, the proportion of strongly structural plants tends to be lower in each stripe, whereas those which have less strong structure or flower earlier are in a larger proportion.

definition of *Echinacea purpurea* and the softer *Filipendula ulmaria*. Too many strong shapes together can make for a planting that seems fussy or restless to most onlookers. Linking plants with small matte-textured leaves and less well-defined forms can be very effective – analogous to creamy-coloured flowers in a meadow, which act as a buffer between stronger colours.

An example of a planting design

The double borders which Piet Oudolf designed for the Royal Horticultural Society garden at Wisley are an example of an innovative and highly complex planting, one whose overall effect is considerably more formal (indeed almost regimented) than what the public have become used to from Piet. The formality is only superficial, however; as one walks down the borders in late summer the predominant impression is that of expansive and untamed perennials. Each side of the border is divided into a series of diagonal 'stripes' containing a plant combination of around three or four varieties.

What is important to realize about this border is that it was designed all at once, not stripe by stripe; it was built up from the top down, not the bottom up. The combination of plants within each stripe has to work together, but the whole has to work together too, and this was the priority in planning.

Planting in time

◄ One of the thrills of the mature garden is that it can develop a life of its own, with established clumps coming back year after year and shorter-lived species regenerating. Here in a well-established border are large heads of *Echinacea purpurea* 'Rubinglow' past flowering and the small red heads of *Sanguisorba officinalis* 'Red Thunder', while the grass is *Molinia caerulea* subsp. *arundinacea* 'Transparent'. On the left at the back is *Aster novae-angliae* 'Violetta'.

Garden and landscape design aims to implement a plan encapsulating a set of ideas and concepts. Unlike architecture and other creative activities that involve inanimate materials, the fulfilment of garden- and landscape-making awaits the growth and development of living things. This leads to questions such as 'when is a garden or landscape finished?' as well as 'what happens when it begins to deteriorate, or develops in ways not originally foreseen?' The fact is that once a garden project is implemented, time is needed for it to mature through growing; those who do not understand this will inevitably be disappointed by the bare appearance of a new garden or landscape. There can be no grand unveiling, like the opening of a building or the dramatic removal of a sheet from a new work of art.

The absence of an obvious moment of completion is perhaps one reason (among many others) as to why many landscape architects use so little planting, or use planting only unimaginatively, relying instead on hard features. They need to show clients a finished project, not one which will still look like an artist's impression in two decades' time.

We see gardens and gardening, and indeed landscape design, as *processes*, not *end results*. Garden*ing* is clearly a process, because it is dealing with living things which constantly change and which need managing. If the plants are not managed, then the garden will eventually become a weed-choked and overgrown wilderness. Even 'wild gardens' or 'wildlife gardens' need managing to preserve their biodiversity, if not their aesthetic qualities. So we argue that as a process rather than an object, a garden cannot be compared to any other product of the artistic imagination – even to those artworks which are designed to decay. A garden is a work of art that is constantly *in progress*.

Seeing a garden as work in progress is the opposite of the way some designers treat a garden as an interior designer would a room in a house which needs a new coat of paint and new furniture. Usually when planning a garden we have a particular look in mind. However, when we have achieved this, even when we are really happy with what we have got, this is no end-product but only a stage, for the gardener will need to work to keep it looking good. Indeed, when gardens have matured to what their owner might consider perfection, they are often at their apogee, and from that point on will begin to decline. It is this life-cycle of gardens that we will consider here, and how it relates to planning plantings.

The ages of the garden

Our ancestors spoke of the seven ages of man. Gardens, too, go through ages, but unlike people, they can be stopped in their tracks and restarted again. Getting the best out of a garden over time involves thinking about its life as cyclical, rather like the endless cycle of birth and death.

IDEA | A garden begins life as an idea. It may be a concept in the mind of an experienced and visionary designer, or just the thought that 'I'd like a lawn and a few flower beds'.

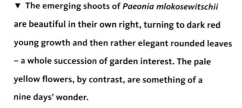

▼ The emerging shoots of *Paeonia mlokosewitschii* are beautiful in their own right, turning to dark red young growth and then rather elegant rounded leaves – a whole succession of garden interest. The pale yellow flowers, by contrast, are something of a nine days' wonder.

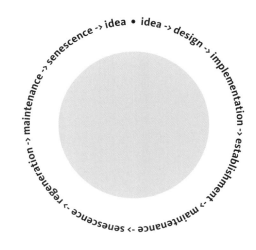

DESIGN | A designer will draw a plan; non-designers will have at least a rough idea in their minds what they want to do.

IMPLEMENTATION | The next step is to turn the design into a physical garden.

ESTABLISHMENT | Immediately a garden is made, it looks raw and empty. As plants grow to fill their allotted spaces and perform the roles desired of them, the garden becomes established. During this time plants may need irrigation, training and extra care with weeding. To ensure short-term interest, some temporary planting of species which develop quickly – and which are often by nature short-lived – may be needed.

MAINTENANCE | When a garden or planting reaches the stage at which its creator is happy and feels that the primary goals have been achieved, it is as near to being finished as any living thing can be. The task now is to maintain it in this desired state.

REGENERATION | With many gardens, however well they are maintained, certain changes occur in the long term to undermine the desired effect. Examples include stronger-growing perennials slowly expanding to form large clumps that oust weaker ones, or trees growing and creating dense shade. A more drastic intervention than general maintenance is needed to restore the balance, which may cause the garden to look rather bare for a year or two, or even longer.

SENESCENCE | A garden may continue to develop without receiving occasional regenerative maintenance. Plants that die may not be replaced, and some may completely overcome others. Whether the skeleton of the old layout remains apparent or the original design intention is unknown, such gardens need restoration. Often they are simply impractical or undesirable for contemporary use and will need a new design. This brings us back to the role of design and planning, for an idea is needed to inspire and give form to the restoration.

Succession – a natural process

As we all know well, bare ground in the garden does not stay empty for long. Nature, you could say, adores a vacuum, and weeds soon start to grow – the beginning of what ecologists call the process of *succession*. The first weeds are usually short-lived plants,

mostly annuals, but they are rapidly followed by perennials. Many of these will also be short-lived, either biennials that live for two years or perennials which live only for three to five years. Over time, however, more long-lived and persistent perennials will establish themselves, grasses in particular. Eventually shrubs and trees start to arrive, and their shade forces out the vast majority of the perennials – a stage which may be reached in only 10 to 20 years. Even among woody plants there is a succession, with trees like birches, cherries and some maples being analogous to short-lived weeds; these fast-growing trees may have a lifespan of less than 50 years, whereas oaks and beech can live for centuries and form the bulk of stable forest communities.

It is useful for the gardener to remember how succession operates, for much of what we do as gardeners is about managing this process so that we effectively stall it at particular stages. For example, weeding a border stops it from becoming a tangle of aggressive weeds and seedlings which would, in the fullness of time, turn it into a forest. Sowing annuals into bare ground mimics the very first years of the succession process, and the appearance of perennial seedlings from other parts of the garden is usually seen as undesirable. The wise gardener and designer also know how to make the most effective use of plants with particular lifespans and life forms.

Co-ordinating the different lifespans of the plants used in a garden or border is one of the greatest challenges facing the designer. Generally speaking, the plants that, in nature, are typical of the first years of the succession process are short-lived, while those that characterize the final stages (known to ecologists as the *climax* plant community) are the longest-lived. Short-lived plants will inevitably tend to die out, longer-lived ones may spread, and in addition as plantings mature and change, the habitat will change too, making conditions unsuitable for some species, forcing them to disappear. The designer needs both to plan ahead and to react to circumstances in order to create a planting that gives pleasure and fulfils its function for many years.

Plant forms over time

Key to the effective use of plants over time is an awareness of how different plants (annuals, perennials and so on) develop and interreact with one another.

Before we embark on this, it is worth remembering the crucial difference between plants that build an above-ground framework which is cumulative (that is to say it is added to every year by more or less permanent woody growth) and herbaceous species, whose above-ground growth dies back in the autumn. Normally gardeners use

▲ It is sometimes possible to combine perennials and annuals. Here, in this late-summer planting, the perennial *Lythrum salicaria* 'Blush' (pink spikes) forms an attractive combination with bronze-leaved *Atriplex hortensis* var. *rubra*. In the background is the low-growing goldenrod *Solidago* 'Goldenmosa'.

the word 'herbaceous' as an alternative to 'perennial'; in fact neither usage is correct botanically – 'herbaceous' describes annuals and biennials as well as the longer-lived perennials, while 'perennial' technically includes trees and shrubs. The importance of the woody/herbaceous distinction for us is that herbaceous plants attain their characteristic height and form very quickly, generally within three years from seed, whereas woody ones may take many years – sometimes decades – to do so.

The form that each species of perennial takes and the speed with which it does so is what makes perennials so useful for gardeners. Time, however, is needed for woody plants to develop both impact and their characteristic form.

• Annuals

Annuals live for one year. In the wild they are mostly either opportunists, growing in bare patches created by animal hooves or landslips, or – and this is true of most of those in cultivation – plants of seasonally dry environments; the individual plants do not survive the long hot summer, but their plentiful seeds will.

Annuals are generally used in dedicated annual plantings – such as those created by the Sheffield School, but can also be used with perennials for creating impact in the first few years, at least if they have relatively light growth which will not compete.

• Biennials and short-lived perennials

Biennials live for two years, generally flowering in the second and producing plentiful seed before dying. In addition there are many short-lived perennials, which may live for three to five years, fling their seed around and die. They are something of a problem to the gardener, because they are very rarely clearly labelled as such! Nor does every reference book advise you that they are short-lived.

The fact that these plants are so free with their seed is their saving grace. Many have great interest as border plants, and the intelligent designer will understand that after the first generation these plants will choose their own positions. The careful gardener will recognize their seedlings and allow them to remain, except when there are so many that they threaten to overwhelm an area, when they will do some 'creative weeding' and thin them out.

In filling gaps, these plants are performing the role that nature designed for them, as opportunists occupying temporary spaces. We can use them for structure or to help create drifts of colour; in both cases, the fact that these plants choose their own positions by self-sowing is a valuable way to design some spontaneity into plantings. Their ability to fill gaps can also be useful in some public spaces which are liable to disturbance and damage.

▲ *Digitalis ferruginea* is one of many plant species which are either biennial or short-lived. Nearly all such plants are profuse self-seeders, but the extent to which they do this is very dependent upon soil and other local conditions.

Alcea rugosa is a rather superior hollyhock. Like nearly all herbaceous members of the mallow family, it is distinctly short-lived, but very easy to raise from seed. ▲

In plantings where long-lived and short-lived perennials are combined, the former will generally oust the latter – indeed, one function of the short-lived species may be to provide temporary interest while the 'permanent' components establish themselves – a horticultural reflection of the natural process of succession. The exception is on very light, dry soils, where drought and low nutrient levels may limit the growth of clump-forming perennials and where seedlings easily establish themselves in the gaps between plants. Here the tendency for short-lived species to produce large quantities of seed gives them a great advantage over longer-lived species, which tend to produce less seed, and so they can remain an element of the design for much longer.

The amount of self-seeding depends very much on the site, and is difficult to predict. The danger is that some species will prove too successful and begin to dominate – this can happen with *Verbena hastata*, for example, which tends to grow right in clumps of other plants. Plants like this can be either vigorously hoed out as seedlings so that only a few survive or removed altogether if they prove too problematic.

Biennials for self-sowing

Agastache foeniculum

Alcea species

Anchusa officinalis

Bupleurum falcatum

Cynoglossum amabile

Dianthus barbatus

Digitalis species

Dipsacus sativus

Eryngium giganteum

Isatis tinctoria

Lunaria species

Lychnis species

Myosotis alpestris

Nicotiana langsdorfii

Oenothera species

Papaver nudicaule

Salvia repens var. *argentea*, *S. sclarea*, *S. sclarea* var. *turkestanica*

Verbascum olympicum, *V. thapsus*

Verbena species

and most umbellifers (*Apiaceae*)

◄ Here a prairie-inspired planting includes the pale yellow *Ratibida pinnata* and the blue-mauve *Agastache foeniculum*, both flowering in mid- to late summer. Both are short-lived perennials – in nature they are 'pioneers', plants which occupy bare ground before being displaced by longer-lived species which form a more permanent plant community. This is the process known as succession.

Given the almost invasive nature of some short-lived species, it is advisable to introduce them at the post-establishment stage unless you have a very hands-on involvement with the garden – perhaps the second or third year is the best time.

Many biennials are particularly valuable for structure, such as umbellifers, digitalis and the thistle-like *Eryngium giganteum*. Others are useful for creating large drifts of colour through their self-sowing activities. *Aquilegia vulgaris* (a short-lived perennial) and its various colour forms (blue, violet, pink, white) is particularly valued for this, and its very light growth is rarely a problem to other plants.

• *Long-lived perennials*
Little attention is given in reference books to the various habits that perennials adopt. A good understanding of how perennials develop over time is a great help in using them more effectively in the garden or public landscape.

SLOWLY DEVELOPING PERENNIALS | Some perennials form extremely long-lived clumps but remain limited in size. Often these are very resilient species, but they can be slow to become established. Examples are *Dictamnus alba*, baptisia and amsonia species. Most of these have strong structure over a long season. When planning and planting borders, care needs to be taken that young plants of these species do not become swamped with other faster-growing ones. They tend to take a year or more to re-establish after transplanting.

STATIONARY PERENNIALS | There are many perennials which probably have a lifespan in the region of five to 15 years, but little research has been done in this area. They do not grow to form clumps, but instead develop a tight knot of stems attached to a persistent, sometimes almost woody, core. They tend to spread through seeding, which can be profuse. Examples are *Salvia nemorosa* and its hybrids, *Knautia macedonica* and *Echinacea purpurea*. Not being able to spread sideways, they are liable to be out-competed by those species which can. Many seem to come from drier environments where there is less competition between plants, and where life is precarious because of drought.

► It might be argued that very vigorous plants are easiest to maintain if they are grown in separate blocks. Here, from front to back, are *Lythrum salicaria* 'Zigeunerblut', yellow *Solidago* 'Goldenmosa' and, at back right, *Eupatorium purpureum* subsp. *maculatum* 'Atropurpureum'. The grass is *Calamagrostis* x*acutiflora* 'Karl Foerster'. This is midsummer.

▼ *Baptisia australis* is one of several prairie species which is slow to establish but immensely resilient and long-lived. Care must be taken in new plantings to ensure that such species are not overrun by faster-growing and more initially aggressive plants.

Pink *Filipendula rubra* 'Venusta' is a strongly growing and competitive plant which forms large clumps. White *Chamerion angustifolium* 'Album' is also a strong spreader – indeed, notoriously so. Putting such vigorous growers together is a good idea – they can

fight it out among themselves, but often end up reaching an attractive state of co-existence. ▼

129

◄◄ A sense of rhythm is created at Pensthorpe by these clumps of *Astilbe chinensis* var. *tacquetii* 'Purpurlanze'. Astilbes are a good example of a perennial which forms slowly spreading solid clumps that tend to eliminate competition over time. The grasses are *Deschampsia cespitosa* 'Goldtau' and *Festuca mairei*.

▼ *Amsonia tabernaemontana* var. *salicifolia* is an example of a long-lived perennial which is tolerant of a variety of stresses but which may be slow to establish.

Rodgersia 'Die Anmutige' does best in lush waterside conditions (but preferably by moving water rather than a still pool), where it grows very vigorously. Put it in less moist conditions and it is more readily out-competed by better-adapted plants. ▼

SPREADING, CLUMP-FORMING PERENNIALS | Most perennials fall into this category, slowly but steadily increasing in size every year through the addition of young shoots around the outer rim of the clump. In some cases, such as *Iris sibirica*, there is no young growth in the centre of the plant, so the plant forms a steadily expanding circle and other species can colonize the central space. Most, however, form a dense mat, regenerating themselves inwardly and outwardly – geraniums and asters being good examples. Clearly, there will be competition when these ever-expanding mats meet, resulting in some perennials' growing at the expense of others. One of the tasks of management is to limit the growth of the more aggressive species. In theory the ability of such plants to keep on growing to form an infinitely large clump means that they are immortal.

It is useful to break down this category further into two categories defined by plant architecture: low clump-formers and upright growers.

• *Low clump-formers*, such as geraniums, hostas, nepetas and many species of stachys, tend to fall into our category of 'filler plants', unless they have particularly strong flower-head shapes or bold foliage and are early-flowering. Many compete strongly early in the year. Persicarias generally have this habit, too, but their relatively large leaves give them extra interest.

• *Upright growers* tend to flower later, have more structural interest and often come from very defined continental climates with a short and intense growing season. They compete with each other by striving to grow as tall as possible. Examples include asters, eupatorium, helianthus, solidago and many other North American perennials. Among grasses, miscanthus is a good example. Plants which combine this habit with a strong production of runners – such as many lysimachias and *Physostegia virginiana* – can be very competitive, effectively excluding other species.

GUERRILLA PERENNIALS | Plant ecologists identify two strategies by which perennials in nature spread vegetatively. In rather military terminology, these are *phalanx* and

guerrilla. In the former case the plant advances on a continuous front, building up a solid clump. With the latter, however, new shoots are sent out some distance from the plant, so that it gradually, or sometimes rapidly, infiltrates its surroundings. The majority of garden perennials fall into the first category, while the latter includes some notorious weeds such as couch grass and ground elder. Some garden ornamentals also have this habit, which can make them somewhat unpredictable – the fern *Matteuccia struthiopteris* is one. Monardas are similar, but their older shoots die out as new ones replace them, making the plants somewhat mobile and liable to be out-competed by species able to establish a more permanent presence.

GROUND-COVERING PERENNIALS | Finally there are those low-growing perennials which can cover quite considerable amounts of ground in a short space of time, generally by using a version of the guerrilla strategy. These are useful for places in shade, where it is difficult to get other plants to grow. They can also be used in new borders to cover the ground between larger and more slowly growing species; as the larger plants establish, they will compete with the ground-level ones, reducing their density. In some cases a balance may be established which is useful for reducing maintenance, with taller perennials emerging from a ground-hugging carpet of shorter ones such as *Waldsteinia geoides* or *Lamium maculatum*.

• *Bulbs*

Many bulbs (or geophytes, to use the technical term which covers plants with underground storage organs: bulbs, corms and tubers) are used for colourful temporary plantings. However, given the appropriate environment, they can be very long-lived elements of the garden. For cool temperate climates, they are particularly useful in borders to provide interest around perennials, most of which in spring are little more than low clumps of green. Selecting bulbs for permanent plantings alongside shrubs and perennials, however, involves selecting species which are both long-lived and unlikely to compete visually and ecologically with other plants.

Early-flowering bulbs (crocus, galanthus, puschkinia, scilla and so on) are often from wild habitats such as woodland and meadow where they experience considerable competition after they have flowered. They not only cope well with rapidly developing perennials around them, or shrubs over them, but also have short-lived and slight foliage which causes no problems, dying away more or less unnoticed. Narcissus varieties, however, although from similar environments, have larger foliage which is very persistent and takes a long time to die, often looking unattractive in doing so. Since it is essential for the health and continued flowering of the plant not to remove this, the bulbs need planting in places where the foliage can be hidden behind other plants such as clumps of perennials. With smaller narcissi this is not too difficult; with large hybrids it can be.

An additional advantage of many of these smaller true bulbs (but not of corms or tubers) is that they are relatively tolerant of disturbance. It is almost inevitable that some bulbs will be dug up accidentally during gardening operations; these small ones seem to be able to re-establish themselves very easily after replanting.

▼ *Camassia cusickii* **is a bulb which will regularly repeat-flower year after year in most gardens and even naturalize in grass. Tulips, however, tend to be less reliable, although this particular variety, 'Queen of Night', is one of the best at reflowering.**

Long-lived geophytes which repeat-flower reliably

W	light shade, woodland conditions needed		*Galanthus nivalis*		G
G	can naturalize in grass; may spread through self-sowing		*Gladiolus communis* subsp. *byzantinus*		
T	will often self-sow and spread in very weak grass under trees		*Hyacinthoides hispanica*		S, I
S	can spread through self-sowing in some circumstances		*H. non-scripta*		S, T
R	sun and reduced competition essential		*Ipheion uniflorum*		
H	many species not hardy		*Leucojum* species		S
I	can be invasive		*Lilium* species: all repeat-flower well but required conditions depend		
			on species; some, including *L. martagon*, *L. monadelphum*		S
Allium: most smaller species		S	*Muscari armeniacum*		R, S
A. hollandicum & other 'drumstick' species		R, S	*Narcissus*: vast majority of cultivars repeat-flower		
Anemone blanda, *A. nemorosa*		W	*N. cyclamineus*, *N. pseudonarcissus*		G, T
Camassia species		G	*N. poeticus* & taller trumpet varieties		G
Chionodoxa species			*Ornithogalum umbellatum*		S, I
Colchicum species			*Puschkinia scilloides*		S
Corydalis cava, *C. flexuosa*, *C. solida*		W	*Scilla* species		S
Crocus species		T	*Tulipa*: reliable cultivars include 'Don Quichotte', 'Negrita',		
Cyclamen species		T, H	'Spring Green', 'White Triumphator'; Darwin hybrids; also		
Eranthis hyemalis		T	*T. aucheriana*, *T. batalinii*, *T. clusiana*, *T. fosteriana* cultivars,		
Eremurus species		R	*T. greigii* cultivars, *T. hageri* 'Splendens', *T. kaufmanniana*		
Erythronium species		W	cultivars, *T. kolpakowskiana*, *T. linifolia*, *T. praestans*,		
Fritillaria meleagris		G	*T. sprengeri*, *T. sylvestris*, *T. tarda*, *T. turkestanica*, *T. undulatifolia*		all R

Many late spring-flowering bulbs are generally from dry habitats, where sparse vegetation results in reduced competition. Such plants do not mix well with perennials and shrubs, and shading often results in their failure to flower the following year. In humid temperate climes they often grow best in gravel gardens or rockeries. Tulips are notoriously reluctant to flower after the first year, a trait shared by the larger alliums if competition is too heavy. However, extensive research in gardens in the Netherlands and Germany, including at Hermannshof, has come up with a healthy number of more promising tulip species and cultivars, as our list shows.

We must not forget the value of growing some of the more vigorous bulbs in grass: some crocus and daffodil species and varieties are very effective used like this. Nor the value of autumn geophytes, such as cyclamen in dry places under trees, or autumn-flowering crocus at border edges and in lawns. Such plants are best used to light up corners empty at this time of year. In some borders, however, there may be too much herbaceous growth by the end of summer for such small plants to be visible.

• *Trees, shrubs and time*

Trees and shrubs dominate many gardens and landscapes in both time and space. Their relatively large size and longevity ensure that they define many green spaces for us, both in terms of what we see in front of us, and also in both individual and collective or historic memory.

We experience different plant forms through time in different ways. One way of visualizing this is to think of layers. Annuals are the most ephemeral layer, and can be changed from year to year, while perennials are the next layer. Their full effect can be realized in only a few years, and since they can be readily dug up, divided and moved around, they are also experienced as dynamic. Shrubs, however, are a longer-term

▲ On dry soils *Eremurus* does particularly well, throwing up dramatic tall spires in early summer every year. Here in the foreground is the Californian poppy, *Eschscholzia californica*, which can start flowering relatively early if it is sown in the previous autumn or has overwintered. This is Home Farm, designed by Dan Pearson.

proposition, often taking the best part of ten years to reach anything like their mature size. The final layer is that of trees, whose lifespan is more comparable to a human lifespan and can be counted in decades, or even centuries. The slowest growers can be planted only as an act of faith in the future, to mature long after those who plant them have passed on. A leap of the imagination is required to have any idea of what they will look like when they are fully grown.

Trees, and to some extent shrubs, are seen by many as permanent. They are not, of course, but their relatively slow rate of growth and the fact that this growth is cumulative means that we tend to see them as always being there, in a way that herbaceous plants, which disappear for the winter, are not. As a consequence, trees tend to define spaces much more in our individual and collective memories. Those who look towards defining space and therefore towards dominating it (mostly men), always like to plant trees. No surprise, then, that landscape architects and landowners use trees alongside buildings to sculpt and define space, often in the process claiming it as their own. Anything else that is planted is all too often seen as secondary and has to fit around them. We would argue that designers should think much more about woody plants and accompanying herbaceous perennials in concert, seeing them as part of an aesthetic system which is designed to be long-lived, with both woody and perennial elements developing together, and inevitably changing together.

• *Trees*

There is little doubt that we have problems in conceptualizing the long lifespan of trees. The fact that their growth is incremental, and slow relative to perennials, means that there is a tendency for them to 'creep up on us'. They grow and suddenly catch us unawares – perhaps when it is no longer possible to see the winter sunset from a

▼ *Cercis canadensis* and its cultivars are immensely colourful North American small trees, tolerant of growing in the company of larger trees and of having perennials planted beneath them.

▼ Birches, such as this *Betula nigra* 'Heritage', are excellent trees for smaller gardens, partly for their size, but also their light shade. However, they have particularly dense root systems which can limit what can be grown beneath them.

▼ *Koelreuteria paniculata* is a medium-sized tree with yellow flowers and interesting bladder-like fruits. It does not compete strongly with underplanting, which makes it good for smaller gardens.

particular window, or the grass starts dying out in ever-deepening shade. Planting a tree is an act that may be the most long-term and large-scale thing that we do. The result may be there, having a considerable impact on the landscape, for a very long time after we are dead. Our opportunities for tree planting are limited (unless you are working in a professional capacity, or have vast acres to fill). It is crucially important that we think through the consequences of our actions in order to avoid joining the innumerable examples of inappropriate tree planting that can be seen in any suburban area – and, indeed, in many country ones.

Trees provide the 'macro' element of a garden or landscape; they also provide continuity, both from season to season and also from year to year. Here it is perhaps useful to consider what trees do not do, and flag up a couple of warnings. Many designed landscapes are composed of little beyond trees and grass, a kind of minimal parkland landscape, which is attractive at first sight, but rapidly becomes boring on subsequent visits. People need and want more interest, which is why shrub and perennial plantings are vital for urban parks and other places where large numbers of people who often have little other access to greenery pay frequent visits. The other point worth making is that trees only *appear* to look after themselves, and that after planting they need some management. Thus when large numbers of trees have been planted, they can require correspondingly greater effort to manage competition between them.

As well as providing continuity through time, trees can provide spatial continuity. This can be particularly appreciated in those cities where there is relatively dense tree planting. The trees not only provide shade and contribute effectively to cool the city during hot summer weather, but also offer a visual linkage from one area to another – a common element that unites different neighbourhoods, balances the effects of adjacent radically different architectural styles and links city to surrounding country. Gardens and parks in rural or edge-of-city locations, in particular, can be blended into their locality very effectively with trees, at least if the trees planted are those that are common locally. In rural areas, particularly, native trees or others which are part of the cultural landscape are very useful for this purpose. The use of so-called traditional trees can be vital for maintaining a sense of local identity and historical continuity.

Small trees to combine with perennials	Shrubs to combine with perennials
Cercis species	*Amorpha* species
Clerodendrum trichotomum	*Aronia* species
Cornus florida, C. kousa	*Broussonetia papyrifera*
Euonymus planipes	*Bupleurum fruticosum*
Hamamelis species	*Caragana arborescens* 'Lorbergii'
Koelreuteria paniculata	*Cephalanthus occidentalis*
Maackia amurensis	*Clethra* species
Paulownia tomentosa	*Colutea xmedia* 'Copper Beauty'
Rhus chinensis, R. typhina	*Comptonia peregrina*
Salix elaeagnos subsp. *angustifolia,*	*Ficus alba*
S. purpurea 'Nana'	*Hedysarum multijugum*
Sassafras albidum	*Hydrangea* species
Sorbus species	*Indigofera* species
Syringa komarovii subsp. *reflexa*	*Kolkwitzia amabilis* 'Pink Cloud'
Tamarix ramosissima	*Lespedeza* species
	Paeonia species
	Rosa glauca
	Salix magnifica, S. moupinensis
	Sambucus nigra 'Gerda'
	Sorbus koehneana
	Syringa species
	Viburnum species
	Vitex agnus-castus

▲ *Acer griseum* is one of many maples suitable for smaller gardens, its relatively small size and light growth helping it to fit in well. However, as with all maples, root competition may restrict what can be grown around its base.

Indeed, they are one of the best ways of tying in a new property or newly developed landscape into its rural or heritage surroundings.

The other side of the coin is that sometimes trees can break continuity. Very alien-looking or prominent trees can stand out from a long way away, and be so dominant that they effectively disrupt the landscape. Examples include palms in rural landscapes in cool temperate climates as well as trees with bright golden or variegated foliage – not only are these conspicuous, but they also have strong connotations of suburbia. The widespread planting of visually prominent trees such as *Robinia pseudoacacia* 'Frisia' or golden-variegated cypresses is another factor in what could be described as a growing homogenization of many areas.

As trees grow their foliage will shade out plants beneath them and their roots will compete for moisture and nutrients. In the case of shrubs this may create unattractive and deteriorating specimens, which will need removal, or replacement with more shade-tolerant species. Perennials will also be limited in their growth, but there are more perennials than shrubs that have coping strategies. We will look in more detail at perennials beneath developing shade in due course.

It is, of course, possible to limit the problem of competition beneath developing trees, either through selection of less-competitive varieties or through the removal of lower branches to create a higher canopy. Prevention is always better than cure, and the former is undoubtedly the best route. Certain smaller trees such as cornus and rowans (sorbus) create less shade and are less competitive, and there are also a great many varieties of other tree species with a narrower crown than the normal forms, which means that they cast less shade – their root competition may not be much reduced, however.

• Shrubs

The role of shrubs in gardens and landscapes is primarily to break up space and create barriers. They are ideal for doing this because of the dense foliage mass they create at eye level. A garden or park composed of nothing but trees and perennials would be very open except for the few months when perennials are tall enough to block our vision. The intimacy of small areas is vitally important for our enjoyment of gardens and our desire to develop a variety of themes within the garden. Shrubs may act as either *physical* or *visual* barriers. Much late twentieth-century landscape shrub planting involved the former – creating massed plantings of shrubs which act as an impenetrable barrier, good for wildlife but often dull to look at. If only a visual barrier is needed, then plantings can be more widely spaced and staggered – with the advantage that the individual character of attractive shrubs is more likely to be appreciated.

Shrubs also provide a transition between trees and ground-level vegetation, and between the wider landscape and the garden or park. This transition can be in the nature of a hedge-like barrier or screen if it is desirable to keep the wider landscape out or a looser barrier where we want to create a sense of openness. Shrubs are also a useful habitat for wildlife, an essential element in the landscape for smaller birds in particular to roost and nest. As ornamentals, they are valued for flowers (mostly springtime), berries in autumn and winter, and for foliage interest – in most cases because of distinctive colour. What a great many shrubs do not have is good or distinctive structure. Most have a very flexible habit of growth and form amorphous masses with time. Exceptions are few: mahonias with large leaves and upright stems, some hydrangeas and aralias which form suckering clumps of upright stems, and, of course, bamboos, which are not really shrubs, but which can be considered in this category as they have a similar range of sizes and can be used to perform many of the functions of shrubs.

Apart from an often all too-brief-flowering season, and in some cases, a somewhat longer late season of berries, the main visual property of shrubs is their foliage. Given

▼ *Cotinus coggygria* (this is variety 'Royal Purple') and *Tamarix ramosissima* both fall into the large shrub/small tree category. The former can be coppiced and so combines well with perennials. *Tamarix* is a light grower and does not compete heavily with underplanting.

Aesculus parviflora is one of several shrubby, suckering chestnut species – most are large trees. Their habit of growth – sending up suckers around the parent plant – does not discourage herbaceous plants, and indeed the combination of young foliage and perennials can be very attractive. ▼

▲ These are the fruits of *Cornus kousa* 'Milky Way'. *Cornus* species are attractive in flower and are good trees for small spaces, offering relatively little root competition.

that they can occupy a large amount of space at eye level, the contribution made by the appearance of their foliage to the overall effect of a planting is major. Broadly speaking, shrub foliage can look relatively low-key or be more emphatic. In many regions, northern Europe and eastern and central North America for example, the majority of native shrubs have small to medium-sized leaves and are deciduous. This means that evergreen shrubs or those with large leaves tend to be read by the onlooker as slightly exotic or alien. Historically, certain evergreen shrubs, such as rhododendrons and so-called laurels (notably *Prunus cerasifera*) have been used extensively in parks and larger gardens. On the one hand this reinforces their non-natural associations, and on the other it creates a strong mental association with deliberately planted landscapes and what we might call a *gardenesque* style where the emphasis is on visually rich but informal planting. Their use therefore might be considered quite inappropriate in situations where a definitely natural look is desired, such as rural locations with a clear heritage value. The low-key shrubs, however, have a relatively demure appearance which enables them to be used anywhere, but might be seen as a bit boring in places where people expect a more visually exciting environment, such as urban or strongly cultural environments.

A useful way of thinking about these issues is to consider a gradient between the low-key and the clearly exotic – exotic here meaning something with an attractively alien aesthetic, rather than simply non-native. The gardenesque look is positioned somewhere between the two:

low-key ←			gardenesque		→	exotic
Amelanchier species	*Hamamelis* species	*Viburnum plicatum*	*Cotoneaster* species	*Rhododendron* species	*Mahonia* species	*Phormium tenax*
shrubby *Prunus* species	*Corylus* species	*Philadelphus* species	*Viburnum tinus*	*Prunus laurocerasus*	*Garrya elliptica*	*Fatsia japonica*

• *Perennials and bulbs under growing trees and shrubs*
Planning and managing space below growing (and therefore expanding) trees and shrubs is one of the most common challenges facing the owners and managers of new and developing gardens. As young shrubs and trees grow, the conditions underneath them change as light, soil moisture and nutrient levels decline.

Some shrubs and trees can have their lower branches removed to allow more light to penetrate to underplanted perennials and bulbs, as well as to improve their visibility. The cyclical growth of wildflowers beneath traditionally managed coppice woodland, where trees are cut on a 20-year cycle, is an interesting model which should inspire us to consider the occasional ruthless cut back. Above all, however, the gardener needs to make use of the tolerance of many woodland-edge plants for varying and changing light levels.

Just how much competition growing woody plants will make for smaller plants beneath them depends a great deal on the conditions. Light, moisture and nutrients are three factors which woody plants limit for things growing beneath them (shrubs

▲ *Anemone blanda* is a bulb of woodland origin which spreads well with time. It goes into early dormancy, so does not suffer from the competition of shrubs and trees in active growth.

This *Ornithogalum nutans* species is a strong-growing bulb for light shade, taking advantage of the early sunlight available beneath deciduous trees. ▲

below trees or perennials below either). As a general rule, if just one of these is lacking but there is plenty of the other two, then there will be no major stress. So, on moist and fertile soils, a surprising number of shrubs and perennials flourish in shade. In most situations, however, there is not enough moisture to make up for what a tree extracts, and so the stress of shade is compounded by the stress of occasional drought. In most gardens it is shade that most limits what can be grown beneath shrubs and trees to those species which have some level of adaptation to coping with shade and nutrient stress. There are great many very attractive woodland perennials and a fair number of shrubs which have these adaptations, but relatively few which can cope with moisture stress as well.

A further limitation for smaller plants growing beneath larger ones on very shallow soils is the fact that the root systems of the larger will be restricted to a shallow plane, thus enhancing the moisture and nutrient stress on anything near them. Naturally thin soils, roof gardens and other similar artificial situations, and areas with high water tables all cause root growth to concentrate in a shallow plane. In these cases only a limited number of shrubs can be combined with perennials. Climate and the availability of moisture during the growing season will also have a major role to play; the more moisture that can be guaranteed during the growing season, the greater the number of perennials which will flourish with shrub competition.

When combining woody plants and perennials the sensible designer looks ahead to the years when competition will increase. Sometimes it may be appropriate to plan to replant, so that once the woody plants have begun to create problems the existing perennials are replaced by ones that are more tolerant of shade and competition. Alternatively, a diverse mixture of adaptable perennials is chosen, so that as conditions become more stressful, those best suited to survival will have the chance to spread, and so to continue to provide interest. Eventually if conditions continue to become difficult, some additional planting of more shade- and stress-tolerant plants will be needed.

So what will such a diverse mixture of perennials include? There are a variety of plant forms and growth cycles which plants have to enable them to cope with shade.

141

But it is not just shade tolerance we are interested in, but also adaptability – if shade builds up, but then there is a drastic prune, how will the perennials react to suddenly greater sunlight? Where cycles of light and shade over many years are likely, then adaptability is vital. An aspect of adaptability is the ability to spread, so that plants can move themselves into new positions as the micro-ecology changes. Several categories can be considered:

BULBS AND OTHER GEOPHYTES | Many of these from woodland habitats (crocus, galanthus, narcissus and so on) grow early, so avoiding the shading of deciduous trees. It stands to reason that they may not be nearly as successful beneath conifers and evergreens. In cool temperate climates the vast majority will flourish in both light shade and full sun, and cope with both some woody plant and perennial competition. Increasing shade will reduce flowering, but the plants will often survive, allowing for growth with renewed vigour if light levels increase. The great disadvantage of most, however, is that they spread only very slowly, tending to build up clumps rather than distributing seedlings over a wide area. There are exceptions, such as *Ranunculus ficaria*.

▼ *Smyrnium perfoliatum* is a very attractive greeny-yellow biennial or short-lived perennial which self-sows enthusiastically in light shade, making it ideal for underplanting where competition from trees and shrubs is not too severe. Its ability to self-sow means that it can adapt to circumstances as they change over time.

Underplanting for shrubs and trees

1   true woodlanders needing humus-rich soil; intolerant of sun and drying out
2   woodland-edge species, tolerant of some sun; intolerant of deepening shade or root competition
3   tough species, able to tolerate deepening shade to some extent and root competition

Perennials

Acanthus mollis 2–3

Aconitum species 2

Actaea species 1

Anemone japonica hybrids 2

Aruncus species 1–2

Asarum europaeum 1

Aster divaricatus, A. oblongifolius 2

Astrantia major 2

Brunnera macrophylla 2

Campanula glomerata, C. latifolia 2

Cardamine species 1–2

Ceratostigma plumbaginoides 2

Chelone obliqua 2–3

Chrysogonum virginianum 1

Convallaria majalis 1

Corydalis species 1

Dicentra species 2

Dictamnus albus 2

Digitalis species 2

Epimedium species 2–3

Euphorbia amygdaloides var. *robbiae* 3

Galium odoratum 3

Gentiana asclepiadea 2

Geranium xoxonianum 'A. T. Johnson',
    G. xoxonianum 2

G. xcantabrigiense 'Biokovo', *G. macrorrhizum,*
    G. nodosum, G. sanguineum 'Elsbeth' 2–3

Gillenia trifoliata 2

Helleborus foetidus 2–3

H. orientalis 2

Hepatica nobilis 1

Heuchera species 1–2

Hosta species 2

Hylomecon japonica 1

Jeffersonia diphylla 1

Lamium species 2–3

Liriope muscari 1–2

Lunaria rediviva 1–2

Mertensia species 1

Molopospermum peloponnesiacum 2

Nepeta subsessilis 2

Omphalodes species 1–2

Pachysandra procumbens, P. terminalis 3

Paeonia emodi 2

Paris polyphylla 1

Persicaria amplexicaulis 2

Phlox species 2

P. stolonifera 1

Podophyllum species 1–2

Polygonatum species 1–2

Pulmonaria species 1–2

Ranunculus aconitifolius 1–2

Rodgersia species 2

Sanguinaria canadensis 1

Saxifraga cortusifolia, S. fortunei 1

Scutellaria incana 2

Smilacina racemosa 2

Stachys officinalis 2

Symphytum species 2–3

Tellima grandiflora 2–3

Tiarella species 1

Trachystemon orientalis 1

Tricyrtis species 2

Uvularia species 1

Vancouveria species 1

Veratrum nigrum 2

Vinca species 3

Waldsteinia geoides 1

Ferns

All 1, except:

Polypodium vulgare 3

Polystichum acrostichoides, P. munitum,
    P. setiferum 2–3

Grasses and grass-like plants

Carex species 2–3

Chasmanthium latifolium 2

Deschampsia cespitosa 3

Hakonechloa macra 2

Luzula species 3

Melica nutans 2

Molinia caerulea cultivars 2

Bulbs and geophytes

Virtually all small bulbs except tulips and
    larger alliums 2

Allium moly, A. ursinum 3

Anemone nemorosa 1

Cyclamen species 3

Galanthus species 3

Trillium species 1

FERNS | The majority need constant moisture as well as some shade, and may not adapt to increasing competition. Some do better than others: *Polypodium vulgare, Polystichum setiferum* and the evergreen *P. munitum* are examples.

SPREADING PERENNIALS | These adapt well as they can react to circumstances. *Brunnera macrophylla*, hostas, many geraniums and lamiums, for example, all spread vegetatively. Digitalis spread themselves around by seed, which is undoubtedly the best strategy for adapting to changing circumstances. Certain more long-lived plants can also spread themselves effectively by seed too, including hellebores and astrantias.

▲ *Cyclamen coum* is a winter-flowering species with a huge variation in leaf patterning and flower colour. It is able to make the most of the light months before trees overhead come into leaf.

WOODLAND-EDGE SPECIES | There are a great many plants which flourish in the borderlands between full sun and shade, with tolerance of a wide range of conditions. Geraniums, for example, flourish in full sun and light shade, but do tolerably well in full shade, so long as root competition is not too severe. Those species which spread effectively, particularly by seed, tend to be 'pioneers', establishing themselves on bare ground or in available spaces for a few generations, before being replaced by longer-lived ones. Such plants are very useful for rapid gap filling and so allow plantings to recover from disturbance. Other woodland-edge plants are much slower to spread and to establish, and are valued instead for being long-lived and persistent. It is possible to draw a gradient between fast-establishing, almost ephemeral species and these longer-lived ones. An adaptable planting needs to have all elements.

pioneering ←————————————————————————————→ **persistent**

most short-lived	reasonably long-lived	long-lived	long-lived as clumps	slow to establish
	very limited vegetative spread	spreading vegetatively	usually spreading vegetatively	some slowly forming clumps
readily self-sowing	readily self-sowing	self-sowing limited	self-sowing rare	self-sowing rare
Bupleurum falcatum	*Aquilegia vulgaris*	*Geranium* species	*Bergenia* species	*Aconitum* species
Digitalis purpurea	*Astrantia major*	*Helleborus argutifolius*	*Hosta* species	*Actaea* species
Meconopsis cambrica	*Helleborus foetidus*	*H. orientalis*	*Pulmonaria* species	*Polygonatum* species
	Lunaria rediviva	*Lamium* species		

Practicalities and maintenance

Members of the gardening public are, quite rightly, critical of discussions of design that avoid tackling practicalities. This becomes quite obvious at lectures when designers talk about their work; many of the questions from the audience are entirely about practical matters. New design concepts, especially where they concern planting, require rethinking of traditional practices – maintenance ones in particular – and it is this that we now address. We consider some general principles, keeping an emphasis on larger-scale perennial plantings, but also look at some specific techniques.

We discuss various practical aspects of maintaining perennial plantings in some detail, but it is important to emphasize that maintenance is not something to be thought about only after a planting plan has been implemented. The level of maintenance and how this is to be achieved in terms of labour and budget are matters to be planned in advance every bit as carefully as the plants themselves are chosen for the site.

Soil preparation

Conventional wisdom sets great store by soil preparation, in particular the 'improvement' of soil by adding composted material, peat and nutrients. We would question whether this is *always* necessary.

Horticulture is historically rooted in the production of fruit and vegetable crops, where the more you put in, the more you get out. The assumption that more nutrients results in better plants has not surprisingly been carried on into the growing of decorative or amenity plants. Much modern research disagrees. Many ornamental plants do not need high nutrient levels to thrive, and there is a danger that an over-supply will only encourage the growth of any aggressive weed seedlings which happen to establish themselves. The focus in contemporary planting design on choosing plants

▶ Traditionally, one of the reasons people clipped shrubs was to show that they were able to afford to pay others to engage in such a time-consuming activity. Nowadays, machinery has speeded up the process, but it still takes time. How much time is going to be spent on maintenance is an important factor to bear in mind in the early stages of garden planning.

▲ The maintenance demands of public plantings are particularly severe and call for careful consideration. Physical robustness, longevity and a long season of interest are all essential. The Battery, New York, planting designed by Piet Oudolf.

for the environmental conditions prevailing at the site recognizes that many highly ornamental plants actually do well on poor soils.

Conventional wisdom also promotes the idea that soil needs extensive preparation by being physically broken up for planting to be successful. This is certainly important for woody plants, which are generally slower to establish than herbaceous perennials, but not, apparently, for perennials themselves. Most perennials grow extensive new root systems every year and are nothing like so slow to establish. In particular they are able to make new growth in unbroken soil more easily than woody plants. Even on heavy clay soils (but *only* when well drained), it is possible to plant perennials with no soil preparation other than digging a planting hole, and when large swathes of planting are involved this can only be described as a boon. Rotovating and other mechanical cultivating techniques can create problems by damaging soil structure and bringing buried weed seed to the surface, so the only advantage of cultivating soil might be where it makes planting an easier and quicker task.

What is vital during preparation is the elimination of as many sources of weed infestation as possible. Weed competition is often the largest problem that new plantings have to cope with, and can be particularly severe in regions with a long growing season. Where a planting is replacing well-established grass, as is often the case in public spaces, there is usually little to worry about beyond the grass itself, which can be either stripped off or sprayed off with a glyphosate-based herbicide. In many large public or commercial projects, the top layer of soil is replaced with sterilized topsoil, guaranteed to contain no weed roots or seeds.

Problems can be severe where the soil holds a large quantity of weed roots or weed seeds. Either may occur in new gardens. Another source is imported topsoil which has spent some considerable time heaped up in storage, growing a nice crop of weeds in the process, all of them leaving their seed behind.

Techniques for dealing with weed roots and weed seeds are different. A variety of non-chemical techniques (such as digging them out) can be used for dealing with perennial roots, but compared with using herbicide these are time-consuming and often ineffective. Using sheet plastic or cardboard to smother weeds can work well so long as no weeds are allowed to grow through holes or at the edges, but this may look unsightly and disposing of covering material can be a problem.

Whereas eliminating weed roots is the end of that problem, buried weed seed is more difficult to deal with in the long term, as a whole new crop of weeds can result every time the soil is disturbed. Traditional techniques for control involve a series of cultivations of the soil which gradually exhaust the weed-seed supply (or the seed bank, as it is technically known) through letting it germinate and then hoeing off or rotovating the seedlings. This process is inherently slow and not always reliable. Sterilizing the top layer of soil with a flame-gun and then planting with as little disturbance as possible is a more reliable option. Chemical treatments which inhibit germination are possible, but have adverse effects on perennials, and in any case the chemicals used are designed to be persistent and are therefore far more likely to result in environmental pollution than standard herbicides. Much commercial landscaping involving shrubs uses geotextile membranes with holes cut for plants; quite apart from

◄ Plants will always have the last say in a design. Some will stay where they are put, slowly expanding the size of their clump, like the grasses here – *Panicum virgatum* and *Molinia caerulea* 'Poul Petersen'. Alternatively, the parent plant may die but be replaced by seedlings, as can sometimes happen with the *Echinacea purpurea*.

The purple-pink *Monarda* 'Scorpion' at the back, like all monardas, will die out in the centre but extend in all directions. It is this kind of plant knowledge which is essential for designers to learn.

the environmental issues around using large quantities of non-biodegradable plastics, this is less suited to the much higher densities of perennial planting. The best solution is probably to replace the top 10–15 cm (4–6 in) of soil with fresh and clean material, so burying seeds below the level of the newly introduced plants. Gardeners tackling large schemes may consider the option of using machinery to invert soils, burying the topsoil (and its weed component) and exposing the upper subsoil. This is also useful if lower fertility levels are required.

Implementing plans

The more complex the plan, the more important it is for the designer to be involved with implementation. Plans involving a high degree of intermingling, in particular, – as opposed to monocultural blocks – generally need the designer to be very much on hand.

Whatever the planting style, it is best to use a grid to break up a large area into more easily dealt with sections. A grid is drawn on the plan, and a corresponding grid laid out on the ground with line; it is then relatively straightforward to delineate plant blocks on the soil with a spray-on marker. Each block is then marked with a stick carrying a label detailing the numbers of plants. Personnel can then deliver plants in the correct quantities to each block, to be set out by the designer.

Plant sizes

Traditionally, herbaceous plants were generally dug up from nursery beds during the autumn and winter and planted out immediately after delivery. Nowadays they are likely to be more readily available in pots. In many ways this is a disadvantage, especially for those involved in planting out large schemes, because 'bare-root' or 'open-ground' plants often offer better value for money because you are not paying for pots and compost, and their attendant transport costs.

▼ Organizing plants before planting is crucially important for large-scale jobs and may require some time on site, even before setting out. Identifying plants while they are dormant, or still very small, requires good labelling.

Here, areas have been marked out with spray paint, to correspond with the designer's drawing, and the plants for each area set out in their planting positions. Now all staff have to do is plant them. ▼

The designer really needs to be there on planting day. No plan can account for all eventualities, and so inevitably there are last-minute decisions to be made. ▼

147

► *Phlomis russeliana* (yellow, right) is one of those plants which seems always predictable and dependable, slowly forming a weed-suppressing clump – making it ideal for low-maintenance situations. The purple in the foreground is *Stachys officinalis* 'Hummelo', the pale grass is *Sesleria autumnalis*, on the left is *Nepeta racemosa* 'Walker's Low'. The red in the background is *Achillea* 'Summerwine'. This is early midsummer.

A variety of sizes is often available with container-grown plants, but the purchase of larger perennials is rarely an advantage; the larger pot sizes are generally intended for the retail trade, where plants have to look good in containers for several months after their purchase from the wholesalers. Very often the plants all started out as the same size the previous autumn, and the plants in the larger pots are the same age as the smaller ones. Once planted out, the smaller ones soon catch up.

With very large projects, or when plants are being obtained from several different sources, it is in practice more feasible to order plants in containers as they can be kept until everything is together and ready for planting – storing bare-root plants is more tricky. Where cost is a major consideration, the propagation of plants by the managers of the project themselves should be considered.

▲ The establishment phase, in the first few years, is crucial to long-term success, particularly the removal of any aggressive weedy species which may arrive.

Planning for maintenance

It is crucial to consider the potential level of maintenance at the planning stage in order to stay within the resources of the owner or manager. In smaller private gardens where the owners are keen and committed this is not usually a problem, but in larger gardens resources have to be spread over more land, and costs can rapidly escalate. With corporate or public clients, maintenance costs are an absolutely fundamental consideration which has to be borne in mind right from the very beginning.

It can be helpful for the designer to approach this issue from of two different angles. In a 'demand-driven' design a planting of a certain kind is wanted, and the designer must assess just how much maintenance it will require. This option is most likely to be encountered with domestic gardeners and clients who want a given result and are prepared to find the resources for its management. Ideally the budget would not be too restrictive, but the designer should nevertheless make a realistic prediction of what tasks will be necessary. The opposite situation arises where there is a limited supply of funding. The designer's brief consists roughly of the statement: these funds are available for maintenance – what kind of planting is possible? This kind of constraint applies to clients who have definite limits on how much maintenance can be afforded – including a great many managers of public space.

However generous or minimal the provisions for its maintenance may be, the ongoing engagement of the designer is crucial for the success of a planting. A competent designer should have an intimate knowledge of the plants chosen, especially of how they can be expected to behave and develop over time. The designer should expect to be engaged to oversee the first crucial years of a planting – when it is becoming established – and subsequently to advise on its development. This may consist of maintaining an agreed standard and keeping the planting static, or allowing it to develop, perhaps in ways that were not foreseen, but which are judged to be acceptable according to agreed aesthetic and functional criteria. The designer should plan to visit twice in the first year, and then to make annual visits, timed to take place in different seasons.

Mistakes or lapses in the first few years of a planting, when young and vulnerable plants are easily lost, can result in gaps later on which can be difficult to fill.

▲ These linden trees (*Tilia* species) have been pruned for a particular long-term effect. Choosing trees which have been appropriately shaped is particularly important in urban or confined environments.

Even in black and white, the structural value of the seedheads of grasses and perennials is high. The old practice was to cut herbaceous plants down once everything had 'finished', but this left only bare beds for winter. Much better to leave the task until late winter. ▲

Herbaceous plants in border-type plantings establish rapidly, usually by the end of the third year in most cases. In plantings such as meadows and prairies, or other plantings where a dynamic and ecological development is expected, and where maintenance is essentially 'extensive' (see below), then establishment can take very much longer. In these cases even if no weeds appear, the constituent elements of the planting will be jostling for position – for ever, in fact; but particularly during the first few years, the possibility of one or two species dominating others needs to be watched. Woody plants can be said to establish within three to five years, but they may well require considerable attention for longer if they need to be clipped or trained into particular shapes. Densely planted trees and shrubs will need inspection and thinning every two years.

Managing ecological processes

Extensive maintenance refers to the management of plantings such as prairies or meadows that are created by sowing a seed mixture. Here everything is treated alike, being mown or cut at the same time; ecological processes are allowed full play, so there is only a limited ability to direct the growth of individual plants or plant species. *Intensive maintenance*, in contrast, refers to the more conventional horticultural practice where plants are treated as individuals. The details of an extensively maintained planting can be expected to change through the dynamic action of ecological process (seeding, spreading, dying), so that the populations and positions of individual plants can be expected to alter from one year to another. Intensive maintenance assumes that plants have fixed positions and need to be kept where they are placed. Much contemporary naturalistic planting can be said to be somewhere in the middle, with changes driven by dynamic processes allowed and encouraged, but only up to a point; intervention to control individual plants may be less than in the conventional garden, but it is still practised, particularly in the early stages. One ongoing role of maintenance in such plantings is to maintain a sense of proportion within the planting, so that there is a harmonious balance between the constituent species.

151

► The private garden of James van Sweden illustrates a planting style which aims to incorporate wild plants with cultivated ones. Maintenance is low and relaxed, so a certain amount of self-seeding is allowed – van Sweden says he wants 'the look of the one that got away'.

As a planting ages, certain species will grow and spread, very often at the expense of others, thus altering the balance. The more extensive the maintenance, the more this is likely to happen. Even in relatively conventional intensively managed borders, changes occur – the difference is that you can decide how much to intervene. Intervention to maintain a balance between species can be represented on a flow chart showing that constant choice between whether to stick to the original conception or to allow a new balance of species to become dominant:

original plan   ←
↓
change in balance
between species   ↑
↓
action to restore   ↑
balance to that of
original plan   →   ↑
↓
or new balance of
species is accepted,   ←
(new community)
↓
change in balance
between species   ↑
↓
action to restore   ↑
balance to that of
new community   →   ↑
↓
or new balance of
species is accepted,
(new community)

▲ Certain plants, for example miscanthus grasses, as in the picture, steadily grow over time to form extensive clumps which eventually will need dividing. Sometimes this happens so slowly that the effects creep up on us, and we suddenly realize that the original design for the planting has now changed. It is up to us to decide whether this is desirable or not.

Some of the best planting combinations are the result of accident, or luck, or nature taking a hand, so to stick to the original plan is often to deny the possibility of exciting spontaneous developments. Besides which, new combinations of plants may develop which are more ecologically stable. Good grounds for intervention are to limit species which have become very invasive and displaced others, particularly where these others have a major impact on the overall visual structure of the planting or are particularly valued for other aspects of their impact. If diversity drops, it may be worth considering adding different species.

With very vigorous species, the following tactics can be used, running from the most drastic to the least drastic:

- Wholesale removal
- Removal of some individuals to limit capacity for future spread
- Reduction of size of clumps
- Removal of all seedlings
- Removal of the majority of seedlings

With very vigorous short-lived perennials and biennials which self-sow a lot, flower-heads or whole plants can be removed after flowering to prevent seed formation.

The large-scale self-sowing of certain species in a planting may sometimes look alarming, but it seems to depend on the species whether they develop into adults or not, and therefore possibly become a problem; only experience can tell, and it is precisely this ability to learn from experience which marks a good manager of plantings. A lot seems to depend upon the scale of plant:

- Species with strong clump-forming vegetative growth (like geraniums) can be problematic in only small numbers.
- Species with large basal leaves (like verbascum species) can be problematic if they self-sow in large numbers.
- Species with upright feathery growth and little clump-forming tendency (like aquilegia and thalictrum) can often build up in large numbers without being a problem.
- Low, ground-covering species or those which develop early (ajuga and *Primula vulgaris* respectively) are rarely a problem, those which tend to become summer-dormant, including these examples, are especially unproblematic.

A phenomenon observed in wild-plant communities is the appearance of large numbers of herbaceous perennial seedlings that do not develop into adults owing to the pressure of competition from established plants. Instead they form carpets of young plants, largely invisible beneath the foliage canopy of their elders. They seem to be able to survive like this for years, developing further only if a nearby vacancy allows competitive pressure to be reduced. Such a situation is to be welcomed, as it shows the development of a strongly functioning ecology.

◄ ► In autumn plants begin to die back. Some of the effects are attractive and colourful, others less so. In smaller gardens selective cutting back can be used to tidy up less attractive elements, leaving those which continue to look good. However, we need to be aware that what is attractive is very subjective, and that perhaps we should open our eyes more to the possibility of beauty and interest in places where we have traditionally not sought it.

Levels of maintenance

As we have said, the level of maintenance a planting receives (and the budget for it) is something that should be decided at the very beginning of a project. Unfortunately, little systematic research into maintenance costs has been done. However, Cassian Schmidt at Hermannshof is recording the person–minutes per square metre required to care for particular perennial-based plantings. Associated with this, he has developed an in-depth analysis of maintenance issues. Our discussion here of maintenance objectives on four distinct levels is partly based on his work:

MINIMAL primarily weed control, occasional mowing, mechanical cutting
    for low-visibility, large-scale plantings, as in public places, wild gardens
REDUCED including cutting back and removal of dead herbaceous growth
    *for low-visibility, large-scale plantings, such as public places, outer areas of
    private gardens*
FULL including staking, mulching, application of compost/manure, control of
    stronger-growing constituent species
    for higher-visibility public plantings, private gardens
OPTIMAL including cosmetic work such as dead-heading and instant removal of
    weed seedlings
    for private gardens

Designers working for many private and public clients will need to establish, in consultation with the client, a set of goals. It may be a good idea for private gardeners to do this as well. Goals will cover not just an idea of what the end result may be, but also how well the maintenance regime will meet a variety of criteria concerned with resourcing (of both money and time), such as the intensity and frequency of work. Very often a designer will need to draw up a set of maintenance specifications for the staff responsible for future management. However, it is vitally important that this is not seen as a rigid and formulaic set of instructions. A designer who revisits the site will be able to amend the specifications as and when necessary, and carry out some staff training. Building up relationships with staff and 'leading from the front' are vitally important if they are to build up a sense of ownership and commitment.

In some instances (very much the worst-case scenario) the client may specify that only a very limited set of operations can be carried out, perhaps on more or less fixed dates every year, by relatively unskilled personnel, with virtually no opportunity for flexibility or direction by anyone with horticultural knowledge. With this kind of rigid schema, only minimal or at best reduced levels will be possible, and the ongoing development of the planting may be seriously compromised. When contractors are used and the planting is not regularly maintained by the same personnel, its future is likely to be very insecure. The best a designer can do is to try to get those responsible for managing the planting to agree to an occasional advisory visit.

With this scenario, most likely to occur in public places, deterioration of any kind of planting beyond the most simple monoculture is likely. Yet if robust species are chosen, it can be surprising how long such a planting can survive. The quality will be low, much lower than in a private garden, but this is not necessarily a problem in public spaces. Roadside plantings are seen by people passing at speed, while in parks the expections of most of the public are so low that anything is better than nothing. In such cases, a cyclical programme of restorative maintenance is realistically more feasible than constant skilled attention. A major effort can be made, every few years, to control weeds and thin out the more rampantly successful perennials under the guidance of the designer or someone with horticultural skill. Alternatively, and this works particularly well in large public spaces, it may be accepted that perennial plantings have a lifespan of, say, between five and ten years, and that once they have become too weed-infested or overgrown they are removed and a replacement created near by, the area of the original planting being returned to mown grass. The costs of doing this will still be much lower than the old-fashioned practice of annual bedding.

Maintenance and ecological strategies

An intelligent strategy for maintenance can be built around the plant survival strategies discussed earlier. Cassian Schmidt relates maintenance clearly to what he calls the 'growth type' of the plants in each area. Growth type is closely related to habitat, and thus to survival strategy. For example, species from dry habitats tend to have small, tough leaves and a compact habit; species from shade to have deep green glossy leaves and a ground-covering habit. Plantings are designed to be related to the particular habitat, so that there is consistency in the growth type of the plants in the various areas of the garden, and maintenance can be planned accordingly. With a knowledge of plant strategies and growth types it becomes possible to plan plantings that will require greater or lesser levels of care, which can be related to different expectations of aesthetic value. For example, vigorously growing plants (typical of moist, fertile soils) will require far more frequent cutting back than slow-growing plants (typical of infertile soils or shade). It cannot be stressed too much how a knowledge of plant characteristics is vital for the implementation of successful maintenance. Key points include:

- Large spaces clearly need more work and need to be planned so that they are maintained with fewer person–hours per unit area. Extensive plantings such a sown meadow or prairie are the obvious solution for the largest areas.
- Stressful environments limit the growth of troublesome weeds and therefore often require much less work. Because annual growth levels are low, the amount of herbaceous growth which is produced, and therefore needs to be cleared away at the end of the season, is also greatly reduced. In shade, for example, grasses and other weeds do not grow well, and shade-tolerant perennials are distinctly slow-growing.

Cassian takes the three survival-strategy divisions of plants – competitors, stress-tolerators and pioneers – and groups different planting styles beneath each one. The following is our adaptation and interpretation, with examples from Hermannshof.

COMPETITORS include robust perennial combinations for sunny or lightly shaded locations, prairie or meadow-type plantings, moist-soil plantings using species of wetland or tall-herb community origin, and woodland edge. The Wisley borders (see page 121) would be an example.

- Robust and vigorous perennials, which vary between rapidly developing types (aster, geranium) and slow, but long-lived ones (paeonia, baptisia), many larger grasses, shrubs.
- For situations where resources (moisture, nutrients, light) are plentiful.
- Main season tends to be early summer to autumn; often good winter aspect with seedheads.
- Plant growth rapidly covers the ground during the growing season, therefore limiting opportunities for weed growth.
- Considerable quantities of herbaceous material produced, which will need removal and composting or shredding and using *in situ* as mulch.
- Competition between species may mean that occasional thinning is necessary to maintain diversity.
- Block planting can reduce the level of management needed to restrict the growth of especially vigorous species.
Maintenance: low to moderate.

Example: Euphorbia and Siberian iris bed, a site with moist fertile soil. Plant remains are cut back in autumn and returned as mulch to the site. Species include *Camassia leichtlinii*, *Euphorbia palustris*, *Geranium pratense*, *Iris sibirica*, *Molinia caerulea* subsp. *arundinacea* and *Persicaria bistorta*. Maintenance averages 10 minutes per year per square metre.

STRESS-TOLERATORS include dry-habitat plantings, steppe, gravel gardens, heather and other acid-soil plantings, Mediterranean-type plantings (maquis-, garrigue- or chaparral-derived), waterside, shade.

- Long-lived, often slow-growing plants. Many bulbs and geophytes.
- In most cases (more nutrient-rich waterside plantings an exception) little herbaceous material produced.
- Environmental stresses limit weed growth.
- Where sub-shrubs are used, a dense mat of vegetation is produced which can be very low-maintenance and attractive – for acidic soils or seasonally hot and dry situations.
- Flowering tends to be spring to midsummer. Many evergreen species.
- Mulching often beneficial, for aesthetic reasons or moisture-retention.

Maintenance: low to very low.

Example: Salvia and achillea planting for dry, stony (including calcareous) soils. Works well with a mineral mulch such as gravel. Plants include cultivars or hybrids of *Achillea filipendulina*, *Knautia macedonica*, *Lychnis coronaria*, *Salvia nemorosa*, *Sedum telephium* and *Verbascum densiflorum*. Maintenance averages 11 minutes per year per square metre.

PIONEERS include high-impact annual and other seasonal or temporary plantings, traditional borders with a large number of short-lived plants.

- Rapidly growing short-lived plants. Often highly decorative.
- Traditional border plantings which rely on visually intense and often very highly hybridized varieties are best included here – annuals, biennials, hybrid perennials.
- For situations where resources (moisture, nutrients, light) are plentiful.
- Generally very high maintenance, as ground has to be kept free of weeds; feeding and irrigation often necessary for best results.
- Low-maintenance annual 'meadow' mixes increasingly available. Maintenance: generally high.

Example: Mallow and artichoke bed. Fertile moist soil with many labour-intensive plants with high visual appeal. Plants include *Cynara cardunculus* 'Cardy', *Foeniculum vulgare*, *Lavatera olbia* 'Barnsley', *Nicotiana langsdorfii*, *Papaver orientale* (Goliath Group) 'Beauty of Livermere'. Maintenance averages 20 minutes per year per square metre.

The success of using this ecological-strategy-guided approach to planning planting is that the appropriate plant selection is used for the environment. This is not an iron rule, but a very strong indicator that unless special measures are taken, the matching of environment to planting palette is the best way to succeeding with plantings which reduce maintenance. For example, the use of a steppe-type vegetation simply for

▼ This combination of drought-tolerant perennials, including varieties of salvia and achillea, is chosen for a dry site, and/or stony, infertile, calcareous soil. In such a situation it will require relatively little maintenance and face little weed competition. However, if used on a moister or more fertile soil, there could well be considerable weed competition because of the relatively open character of the planting.

▼ In general perennials thrive on deep fertile soils, with good summer-long levels of moisture. Cutting them back in the winter is the main task of the year, but once established their vigorous growth minimizes the dangers of competition from weed seedlings.

aesthetic purposes on a fertile moist soil is asking for trouble, as the open character of the vegetation will invite the invasion of weed seedlings. However, it may well be possible if certain other conditions are met, for example if the steppe plants are grown through a thick layer of gravel (minimum 7 cm or 3 in). Alternatively, fertile topsoil may be stripped off and used elsewhere, and dry-meadow species or other species of poor soils planted or sown into the subsoil, as is common practice with European wildflower-meadow seed-mix sowing. Another way of looking at this is to say that matching vegetation to environment is the most sustainable way of designing plantings. Environment can be defied only if inputs are increased – in terms of labour, costs and, arguably unsustainable, inputs of chemicals, quarried gravel, irrigation and so on. For a full discussion of this, see Schmidt and Hoffmann (2003).

Maintenance tasks

SUPPORTING | Staking is one of the essential summer tasks in traditional borders, but is much reduced with modern plantings. Many highly bred cultivars need supporting with stakes because their disproportionately large flower-heads overload the stems. Traditional feeding often makes plants grow unnaturally large, too, or develop soft, sappy stems. The species popular in contemporary plantings are generally either wild species or cultivars close to the wild, with the natural proportion of flower to stem.

A few plants always seem to need support, however, and in certain conditions – a wet summer, wind, light shade – other generally upright species may sometimes need it. In the Oudolf garden in Hummelo, with some 3,000 square metres or yards of border, only three to five hours a year are spent inserting supports. The half-round hoops 1.4 m (4 ft 6 in) high that they use are simple to insert and less time-consuming than canes and twine.

Recent years have seen the emergence of more artistic styles of staking and support using hazel and willow. Where staking is vital, whatever the reason, this may be a way of turning a problem into an asset. As a general rule, staking is more important in a small area where flopping plants are more likely to be conspicuous than in larger areas.

SUMMER PRUNING | Some gardeners have always cut back certain perennials to control their growth. Tracy DiSabato Aust, working in the American Midwest, has carried out a great deal of research into this issue, described in her 1998 book (see Bibliography). She has shown how it is possible to not only reduce the height at which many taller perennials flower, so making them more manageable, but also to produce more flower, often on bushier stems, so enhancing the ornamental aspect of the plants. The technique is undoubtedly useful in small gardens, and can also be employed as an alternative to staking. Flowering is often delayed, but only by a short time.

The technique works in a continental climate with hot summers and plentiful moisture. It is certainly less reliable in climates where there is no guarantee of summer moisture, or where cool weather may reduce the pace of growth. It is, however, worth experimenting.

▲ *Helianthus salicifolius* is an example of a very tall perennial which generally does not need to be staked when it gets older. Its main appeal is not its small yellow flowers, but the fine and rather floppy leaves on the soaring stems.

Some early-flowerers like geraniums and *Salvia nemorosa* varieties can be cut back in midsummer in all climates and will often flower a second time in late summer, but the danger of doing a lot of cutting back is that too many bare plants will detract from the attractiveness of a planting during mid- to late summer. (See page 104 for a discussion of dealing with plants after early summer flowering.)

FEEDING | Conventional garden practice has tended to support the idea that high fertility is not only good, but necessary. But anyone looking at the display of dry-meadow or steppe wildflowers which can grow on little more than shattered limestone in many mountain or hill regions will understand that this is not the case. High fertility can sometimes be counterproductive – overfed plants are more likely to topple over or to fall victim to fungal disease.

While it is perfectly possible to plant up a poor soil with an array of species that will look good and thrive, many gardeners want something more. Any lover of perennials, especially the later-flowering ones, from fertile prairie or tall-herb habitats, will feel frustrated if they live on a light sandy soil or other low-fertility situation. Feeding then becomes an important issue. In line with general horticultural practice, the important thing is to build up the organic matter of the soil, as a good humus content will not only hold both nutrients and moisture, but also make them available to plants. Well-rotted organic matter needs to be added to the soil at planting time and an annual mulch applied. Extra nutrients are best and most economically supplied by using organic-origin slow-release fertilizers.

Once established, plantings can have nutrients recycled – see below under 'cutting back'.

In meadow and prairie habitats, a key role is played by legumes, a family characterized by root nodules containing nitrogen-fixing bacteria that convert atmospheric nitrogen into soluble nitrates which plants can use. It is quite possible that such plants could play a similar role in garden plantings, although we know of no research that has been done to date. Attractive members of the family that could be used, particularly for later-season or prairie-type plantings, include yellow thermopsis species for early summer, baptisias for midsummer and desmodiums for late summer. For smaller-scale plantings there are increasing numbers of smaller members of the family becoming available, such as trifoliums, lathyrus and others.

CUTTING BACK | The cutting back of dead herbaceous material is a key end-of-season task. There is no 'right' time to do this: it is very much an individual decision. Dead seedheads are certainly an important wildlife resource, either for food or to harbour overwintering insects. They can be very beautiful, too.

The aesthetic appeal of a garden of deadheads depends partly on the species mix and partly on weather. Plants vary enormously in how well they stand. As a general rule, grasses are resilient enough to be still looking good by late winter, but flowering perennials vary much more widely in their ability to stay upright. Only a few can really complement the grasses by the end of the winter, with some collapsing into a dark mush with the first frost. High rainfall combined with wind is the worst-case scenario

▶ Bright and clear winter skies have a particularly sharp light which can work magic on the faded and bleached remains of perennials in the last few weeks before they are cut back. These are the remnants of echinacea seedheads, long since picked clean of seed by hungry birds.

162

163

for autumn, apart from an early snowfall that flattens just about everything. A dry and quiet autumn, however, can see borders full of perennial seedheads glowing in low sunshine in every shade of fawn, yellow and brown.

One policy for cutting back is to do it in stages, removing plants which look a mess and leaving behind those which still have good structure until late winter – before the first bulbs of spring begin to emerge.

What to do with the cut material? Large quantities can be generated, especially by lots of late-flowering species, many of which develop substantial and tough stems. Alternative ways of dealing with this material are to shred it and use it as a mulch, or to compost it.

Composting requires space for a heap, and room in which to turn it; with the volume of material produced, this can mean giving over more space than the owners of small gardens may wish. Once composted, the result can be used as a mulch on the soil around the plants, so returning nutrients to the soil, or it can be used elsewhere, on the vegetable garden for example – in which case we can think of this as transferring nutrients from one part of the garden to another.

Shredding is the best way to deal with the hard stems of large grasses such as miscanthus and of flowering perennials such as macleaya, eupatorium and vernonia. Any shredder seems to be able to deal with this kind of material, although progress is slow with smaller models. Problems arise with softer material, such as finer stems and soggy leaves, which rapidly clog most machines. Advice should be sought from suppliers of machinery and ideally you should trial a model before committing yourself to buying. Shredded material may be added to the compost heap – it will break down much more rapidly than unshredded – or applied as a mulch to the soil surface, again returning nutrients. Material shredded this way is generally left as lengths of 2 to 3 cm (about 1 in), and looks tidy enough as a mulch.

In large gardens or public landscapes the best way to deal with dead herbaceous material is with a brushcutter or a hedgetrimmer fitted with an arm to be used near ground level. If plants are cut downwards from the top of the stem, the material is effectively shredded and can be left in place as a mulch. The results are too untidy for the taste of most small-garden owners, however, as stems are always much longer than when they are cut with a shredder and are scattered widely.

MULCHING | In addition to shredded or composted dead herbaceous material, other material may be used as a mulch for a variety of purposes. Garden compost or other decayed organic matter may be applied as a way of adding humus or nutrients to the soil. Worms and other soil denizens will drag material down under the surface, and adding material in this way is very effective at encouraging a healthy soil fauna and structure.

Mulches of undecayed organic matter may also be applied – as it decays it too will benefit the soil. What is available depends very much on what local agricultural industries produce as a waste product.

All mulches help reduce moisture loss if applied while the soil is still damp, and help to reduce the germination of weed seeds. The most effective suppressant of weeds,

▲ After the big winter clear-up and cut-back, gardens can seem bare, but this is necessary in order to set the stage for spring. Some people find the open and empty character of the late-winter garden quite attractive, perhaps as a contrast to the fullness and exuberance of the rest of the year.

though, is a 5 cm (2 in) layer of 1 cm (½ in) chipped bark – a commonly available waste product of forestry operations. Its advantage is that it decays slowly, so can last for several years, and presents an attractive surface, at least if medium rather than coarse grades are used. Fine grades are less effective at preventing weed-seed germination. It should not be allowed to become mixed in with soil, as it will rob the ground of nitrogen as it decays, and it should be used only if already partly composted, as some fresh wood/bark chip releases toxins which can damage young herbaceous growth. The addition of a slow-release source of nitrogen (such as hoof and horn) will help to reduce the denitrification problem.

Old newspaper, either shredded or used in sheets, is an effective mulch, especially for conserving moisture, and looks perfectly respectable if covered in compost or decorative mulch.

Mineral mulches, such as gravel or lava, are appropriate for dry-habitat plantings; they fulfil many of the functions of wood-based mulches, but look more appropriate with these plants.

WEED CONTROL | This is the big one! More than anything else, weeds threaten the aesthetic and often the ecological integrity of plantings. Since nature-inspired plantings tend to look untidy and 'weedy' to some people, we should perhaps discuss what is meant by a weed. The popular saying is that 'a weed is a plant in the wrong place'. This evidently depends very much on the situation, and we shall argue that many plants which some might define as weeds should not always been seen as such. In addition, some garden plants can be too successful and spread invasively or self-sow so extensively that they become weeds. In terms of ecological survival strategies, most weeds are pioneer plants or competitor-types. They grow so fast that they tend to swamp the desired plants, and generally reproduce rapidly. Particularly problematic are:

• Young plantings, where desired plants are small and vulnerable.
• Maritime-influenced climates with a long growing season, where local weeds are able to grow for much longer periods than winter-dormant perennials. Early spring is a particular window of opportunity for weeds.
• Regions which have a serious problem with invasive aliens.

Weeding techniques include hoeing, hand-pulling, and appllication of herbicides.

• *Hoeing* In spring, before most perennials have emerged, seedlings are easily hoed off, preferably on a dry day so they rapidly desiccate.
• *Hand-pulling* After early summer, the vegetation canopy should have closed up – making one of the best defences against weed-seed germination. From now on, it is mostly tall weeds which penetrate the canopy that cause a problem. Hand-weeding is the most practical way of dealing with these, although care needs to be taken not to cause damage as you walk through the planting.
• *Herbicides* Once plantings are established and reasonably well maintained, physical

167

◄◄ Large perennials can be a magnificent sight in autumn. The grass on the right is *Miscanthus sinensis* 'Flamingo', while the distinctive globe-shaped seedheads belong to *Phlomis tuberosa*. Once they are to be cut back, a decision must be taken as to what to do with the remains. Shredding and returning to the bed as a mulch is the most ecological solution, as it recycles nutrients.

▲ The danger of alien invasive plants escaping from gardens is a real one, but the risks need to be looked at rationally and based on knowledge and science, not ill-informed headlines in the newspapers. Waterside plants such as this *Petasites japonicus* are a particular known risk in many regions, because of the ease with which water transports plant fragments downstream. Many waterside plants are also very vigorous.

means of weed control should be sufficient. Problems can sometimes occur, however, especially if preparation of the site was inadequate, or problem species get blown in on the wind.

Chemical weed control is now regarded by many as undesirable. However, we believe that this is an issue that needs to be looked at rationally, not dogmatically. Many organic practitioners willl admit (in private, never in public) that they would *only* recommend adopting an organic management policy *once all weeds have been eliminated from a site* – they recognise that chemical weed control is often the only realistic way to remove persistent perennial weeds. Once weed clear however, it is possible to adopt purely physical means of control, even in large gardens, and possibly, if there is enough commitment to staff training, at the level of the municipality.

However the reality though, sometimes aggressive problem weeds re-establish themselves, and at any level above that of the small garden, there may be real problems with having enough time, or staff, to control them. Weed incursion causes two problems which steadily build up over the years: one is a loss of visual appeal, which in the case of large gardens managed by professional staff or public gardens, means a loss of client support, and a loss of biodiversity – as an area dominated by a small number of weedy species will have much less interest for wildlife than one with a rich flora, especially if the weeds concerned are invasive aliens. This is when it may be necessary to resort to herbicides, in effect to save the planting. Since there is, however, little evidence that the biodegradable herbicides now available for sale in a very strictly regulated market (for example, glyphosate-based) pose any real threat to either the environment or human health if properly used, *and* since we do not believe that the plantings we promote have any need for other synthetic chemicals such as insecticides or fungicides, we do not see why we should be made to feel guilty about doing so!

Public concern is likely to be reduced if those engaged in management using herbicides are seen to be using them responsibly, and argue the case for using them. Professionals who use herbicides have to work within a strict regulatory framework – amateurs who use them would do well to use similar procedures. Local agricultural advisory services or agrochemical suppliers should be able to supply information.

Robust, long-lived perennials and ferns

These are useful for public spaces and less intensively maintained gardens:

Acanthus species

Aconitum species

Actaea species

Amsonia species (long-lived, but slow to establish)

Anemone xhybrida

Aralia species

Artemisia lactiflora

Aruncus species

Aster cordifolius, *A. divaricatus*, *A. ericoides*, *A. novae-angliae*, *A. oblongifolius*, *A. tataricus*

Astilbe species

Astrantia species

Baptisia species (long-lived, but slow to establish)

Brunnera macrophylla

Ceratostigma species

Chelone species

Clematis: herbaceous species

Dalea purpurea (long-lived, but slow to establish)

Darmera peltata

Desmodium species

Dianthus carthusianorum

Dryopteris species

Echinacea species

Echinops species

Epimedium species

Eryngium species

Eupatorium species

Euphorbia amygdaloides, *E.* EXCALIBUR 'Froeup', *E. griffithii* 'Dixter', *E. palustris*, *E. polychroma*, *E. schillingii*, *E. wallichii*

Filipendula species

Geranium sanguineum, plus all species over 30 cm (12 in) tall

Gillenia trifoliata

Helenium species

Helianthus species

Helleborus species

Hemerocallis species

Inula species

Iris sibirica

Kalimeris incisa

Kirengeshoma palmata

Ligularia species

Limonium platyphyllum

Lobelia siphilitica

Lychnis chalcedonica

Lysimachia species

Lythrum species

Maianthemum racemosum

Nepeta xfaassenii, *N. racemosa* 'Walker's Low', *N. subsessilis*

Origanum laevigatum & hybrids

Osmunda species

Paeonia species

Papaver orientale

Patrinia scabiosifolia

Perovskia atriplicifolia

Persicaria species

Phlomis russeliana, *P. tuberosa*

Phlox paniculata cultivars

Polystichum species

Pycnanthemum species

Rhazya orientalis (long-lived, but slow to establish)

Rodgersia species

Rudbeckia species

Salvia nemorosa, *S. xsylvestris* cultivars

Sanguisorba species

Scutellaria species

Sedum species

Silphium species

Solidago species

Stachys species

Strobilanthus atropurpureus

Succisella inflexa

Symphytum species

Thalictrum species

Trifolium rubens

Trollius species

Uvularia species

Vernonia species

Veronica species

Veronicastrum species

Zizia aurea

Robust and resilient grasses

These are robust, but until they flower are so similar to wild grasses that they will be mistaken for them by untrained maintenance personnel:

Briza media

Calamagrostis species

Eragrostis spectabilis

Melica species

Poa species

These grasses are more distinctive to the untrained eye:

Carex species

Deschampsia species

Festuca species

Hakonechloa macra

Luzula species

Miscanthus species

Molinia caerulea subspecies & cultivars

Panicum species

Sesleria species

Spodiopogon sibiricus

Stipa gigantea

Bibliography

Literature

Brookes, John. 1988. *The New Garden*. London: Dorling Kindersley.

Diekelmann, John, and Robert M. Schuster. 2002. *Natural Landscaping: Designing with Native Plant Communities*, 2nd ed. Madison: The University of Wisconsin Press.

DiSabato-Aust, Tracy. 1998. *The Well-Tended Perennial Garden: Planting and Pruning Techniques*. Portland, Oregon: Timber Press.

Dunnett, Nigel, and James Hitchmough, editors. 2004. *The Dynamic Landscape: Naturalistic Planting in an Urban Context*. Abingdon: Spon Press.

Föhn, M. 2004. Die Mischung macht's – Integrierte Pflanzstysteme. *Garten + Landschaft*, October.

Grime, J. P. 2001. *Plant Strategies, Vegetation Processes and Ecosystem Properties*. Chichester, UK: John Wiley.

Hansen, Richard, and Friedrich Stahl. 1993. *Perennials and Their Garden Habitats*. Cambridge, England: Cambridge University Press.

Kendle, A. D., and J. E. Rose. 2000. The aliens have landed! What are the justifications for 'native only' policies in landscape plantings? *Landscape and Urban Planning* 47: 19–31.

King, Michael, and Piet Oudolf. 1998. *Gardening with Grasses*. Portland, Oregon: Timber Press.

Kingsbury, Noël. 2003. *Natural Gardening in Small Spaces*. Portland, Oregon: Timber Press.

Kingsbury, Noël. 1996. *The New Perennial Garden*. London: Frances Lincoln.

Oudolf, Piet, and Henk Gerritsen. 2003. *Dream Plants for the Natural Garden*, Portland, Oregon: Timber Press.

Oudolf, Piet, and Henk Gerritsen. 2003. *Planting the Natural Garden*. Portland, Oregon: Timber Press.

Oudolf, Piet, with Noël Kingsbury. 1999. *Designing with Plants*. Portland, Oregon: Timber Press.

Owen, J. 1991. *The Ecology of a Garden*. Cambridge, UK: Cambridge University Press.

Schmidt, C. 2004. Die Steppe kommt. Trends bei der Pflanzenverwendung. *Garten + Landschaft*, October.

Schmidt, C., and T. Hoffmann. 2003. Dauerhafte Staudenpflanzungen. *Grün Formula* (August).

Wasowski, Sally. 2002. *Gardening with Prairie Plants: How to Create Beautiful Native Landscapes*. Minneapolis: University of Minnesota Press.

Wiley, Keith. 2004. *On the Wild Side: Experiments in New Naturalism*. Portland, Oregon: Timber Press.

Web resources

More information on gardens, designers and projects can be found on the following websites:

USA
The Battery Conservancy New York
  www.thebattery.org
Chicago Botanic Garden
  www.chicagobotanic.org
Roy Diblik, Northwind Perennial Farm
  www.northwindperennialfarm.com
Gustafson Guthrie Nichol Ltd
  www.ggnltd.com
Millennium Park Chicago
  www.millenniumpark.org
The Morton Arboretum
  www.mortonarb.org

UNITED KINGDOM
Noel Kingsbury
  www.landsol.com
Pensthorpe
  www.pensthorpe.com
Dan Pearson
  www.danpearsonstudio.com
Royal Horticultural Society's gardens at Wisley
  www.rhs.org.uk
Scampston Hall and Walled Garden
  www.scampston.co.uk

NETHERLANDS
Piet Boon
  www.pietboon.nl
Piet and Anja Oudolf
  www.oudolf.com

LUXEMBURG
Altlorenscheurerhof
Information through:
  pauline.mcbride@invik.lu

GERMANY
Hermannshof Garden
  www.sichtungsgarten-hermannshof.de

SWEDEN
Stefan Mattson, Enköping
Information through:
  parker@kommun.enkoping.se
  or: www.enkoping.se

SWITZERLAND
  www.unr.ch
for information on the integrated planting system look on this website, following the links F&E; Projekte; Entwicklung Integrierter Pflanzsysteme

Acknowledgements

Piet Oudolf

Among the many people I'd like to acknowledge are British garden designer Dan Pearson and Roy Diblik from Northwind Perennial Farm in Wisconsin who inspired me with his love for North American natives. I'd also like to thank all those people who have commissioned work and with whom I have worked, including:

Kathryn Gustafson and partners from Seattle and Robert Israel – we did the Lurie Garden together in Chicago; Warrie Price from the Battery Conservancy and her team who gave me my first assignment in New York; Piet and Karin Boon, house and interior designers from Oostzaan, The Netherlands; Sir Charles and Lady Legard at Scampston Hall in Yorkshire; Bill Makins who commissioned me to design the garden Pensthorpe; John Coke who through his love for plants gives the garden I designed for him at Bentley in Hampshire an extra dimension; The Royal Horticultural Society for their support in creating two immense long borders in their gardens at Wisley.

I would also like to thank the following people who make sure the gardens are preserved for the future: Colin Crosbie, Wisley; Stefan Mattson, Dreampark, Enköping; Colleen Schuetz, the Lurie Garden, Chicago; Sigrid Gray, The Battery, New York; Paul and Pauline McBride, Altlorenscheuerhof, Luxembourg; Tim Marshall, Scampston Hall, Yorkshire; and Ed Uhlir and his team for working with all of us on the Lurie Garden.

I also thank Anja, my wife and partner, for her everlasting help in the background and in running our small nursery.

Noel Kingsbury

I'd like to thank and acknowledge all those people who have contributed to the exciting melange of ideas which is contemporary planting design. In particular I wish to thank Cassian Schmidt of the Hermannshof garden in Weinheim, Germany, whose hospitality and whose enthusiasm for sharing his innovative ideas have been among the most interesting and stimulating aspects of my research over the last few years.
Other designers and gardeners whose work has been an inspiration include Keith Wiley, Mary Payne and James van Sweden.

It is also worth mentioning a number of others with whom I have been working since Piet and I last did a book together. An attachment to the Landscape Department at the University of Sheffield has meant that I have been focusing much more on a scientific approach to how plants can be grown and combined. Working with my research supervisors, Nigel Dunnett and James Hitchmough, has been very informative, as have discussions with other post-graduate students working in similar areas – Cruz Gaali, Linli Dao and others. I'd also like to thank those who have given me opportunities to create plantings in public spaces in Bristol, notably Graham Evans and Jon Bown.

I'm very grateful to Sue Berger and Deb Evans for reading through the manuscript and making various comments and suggestions. Finally, thanks to Hélène Lesger at Terra and Anna Mumford at Timber Press for making this project happen and to my partner, Jo Eliot, whose belief in me and my work I appreciate so very much.

Index

175

Picture Credits

Cassian Schmidt
19 lower right, 27 below, 29, 31 below, 40, 44 upper right, 46, 47, 79, 80-81, 101, 125 upper right, 128, 158

Jane Sebire
31 above

Jo Withworth
86

Marianne Majerus
66 upper left, 73, 76-77, 85 upper right, 102, 103, 105 upper left, 129 below, 148-149, 159

Mark Bolton
30, 32

Neil Holmes
8, 89 below, 90 upper right, 130-131

Nicola Browne
10 below, 14-15, 20, 26 upper right, 33, 94 upper left, 95 upper left, 96, 110-111, 117 upper left, 145, 147 upper left, 151 upper left, 152

Noel Kingsbury
28

Piet Oudolf
6, 9, 10 above, 11, 12, 13 lower right, 16, 17, 19 lower left, 21, 23, 25, 26 upper left, 27 above, 34, 37, 38, 39, 42, 43, 44 upper left, 48-49, 50, 51, 52, 53, 56-57, 58, 60, 61, 62, 63, 69 below, 72, 74, 75, 85 upper left, 85 lower left, 87 above, 89 upper right, 90 upper left, 91, 92-93, 94 upper right, 95 lower right, 97, 100, 104, 105 below, 107, 108, 109, 112, 113, 114, 115, 116 below, 117 upper right, 118-119, 120, 122, 123, 124, 125 upper left, 126, 127, 129 upper left, 129 upper right, 132, 133, 135, 136, 137, 138, 139, 140, 141, 142, 144, 146, 147 below, 150, 151 upper right, 153, 154, 155, 160, 164, 166-167, 168

Sabina Rüber
45, 88

Walter Herfst
jacket, cover, 13 lower left, 18, 54, 64-65, 66 upper right, 69 above, 70-71, 84, 87 below, 89 upper left, 116 top, 162-163

The pictures of Piet Boon's garden made by Nicola Browne are reproduced with kind permission of *Gardens Illustrated*.

COLOPHON

© Text: Piet Oudolf and Noel Kingsbury
© Design and layout: Terra Lannoo Publishing, The Netherlands
All rights reserved.

Published in the English language in 2005 by
Timber Press, Inc.
The Haseltine Building
133 S.W. Second Avenue, Suite 450
Portland, Oregon 97204-3527, U.S.A.
www.timberpress.com
For contact information for editorial, marketing, sales distribution in the United Kingdom, see www.timberpress.com/uk.

Published as *Planten voor morgen* in the Dutch language in 2005 by
Terra Lannoo, The Netherlands,
www.terralannoo.nl, info@terralannoo.nl

ISBN-10 0-88192-740-6
ISBN-13 978-0-88192-740-5

Graphic design by Gert Jan Slagter
Printed by Toppan, Hong Kong

A catalogue record for this book is available from the Library of Congress and the British Library.